THE DAY I THREW BANANA BREAD AND ALMOST WENT TO JAIL

True Stories About How I Used to Lose My
Temper (and How I Learned to Stop)

Jeanette Hargreaves, M.Div.

The Day I Threw Banana Bread and Almost Went to Jail: True Stories About How I Used to Lose My Temper (and How I Learned to Stop)

Copyright © 2020 by Jeanette Hargreaves, M.Div.

Published by Jeanette Hargreaves, LLC

Ebook ISBN 978-1-0878-8258-1

Print ISBN 978-1-0878-8247-5

Library of Congress subjects: Parenting | Success

For Mom and Dad,

God rest your souls. You did the best you could.

Table of Contents

PART II: Emotional Intelligence at Home

Dear Reader,

When I talk about the work I do, I say, "I help moms who lose their temper. I used to yell at my kids every day, but I got help, and now I help others." Depending on who's listening, I get two reactions.

The first reaction is a sideways look. They look at me with surprise and suspicion. They're thinking, "C'mon. Do you really NOT yell at your kids?" In other words, "Are you for-real?" They don't believe me. For them, that's the way life is. Kids get yelled at. It's normal. It's necessary. Some of them even say to me, "Wow, doesn't everyone yell at their kids? You must have a big business."

The second reaction is a different kind of wow, "Wow, you must have a pretty small business. I only know one person like that."

I feel like I'm standing between two big bubbles. There's the bubble where people yell at their kids (and do other things, like throw banana bread), and then there's the bubble where they don't. I'm here to tell you the good news—that I broke out of the bubble where people yell at their kids, and you can too.

I have just one question: Are you ready?

Because I'm going to tell you all the juicy stories. I'll tell you the details about the day I threw banana bread, and

I'll also talk about the day I screamed at my daughter for dumping a container of bubbles on the ground. I'll even tell you about the most recent day where I didn't yell, but I cussed at the kids (I'm still working on all this stuff!).

And, sister, I'm holding out my hand to you (yes you, dear reader). It's an invitation to go on this journey with me. I'll walk with you step by step while I show you how I broke out of the bubble, and how I'm still working on staying out.

There's a part of me that can't explain how or why I woke up one day and decided that I had to take action and stop the yelling in my house. There was just something about it that didn't seem normal, that didn't seem right. And I wondered, "Is all this yelling necessary?" This is my story.

I wrote this book in two parts. In Part I, I'll tell you stories about how I used to yell and how I learned to stop yelling. In Part II, I'll tell you stories about how I discipline the kids now and teach you how to do it. Part II has the scripts, like what to say when your kid lies to you, or what to do when they hit another kid. As I've been teaching, these are the scripts moms ask me for. Let's begin.

PART I

How I Broke the Yelling Habit

Chapter 1

The Day I Threw Banana Bread

The day I threw banana bread was one of my rock-bottom moments. It was July 3rd. As a caregiver for my dad, I filled many responsibilities, including responsibility for his happiness. Yes, as crazy as it seems, as an adult, I felt entirely responsible for my dad's happiness. I already had plans for the 4th of July with the kids and the in-laws. Those plans didn't include Dad, and I worried for days about how his feelings could be hurt.

I thought to myself, "Dad needs a party too."

So I planned it for July 3rd. I pictured Dad sitting on my back porch with an iced tea enjoying the holiday. I bought sparklers for the kids to run around with in the backyard. I wanted Dad to enjoy his grandkids as part of the fun. I also invited the neighbors and the in-laws. This was going to be a sweet little party.

On the 3rd, Jeff (my dear husband) got on the grill to cook up some hamburgers and hotdogs—classic July party food for Texas. I baked not one, but two sour cream peach pies. It's the kind of pie that tastes like southern American sunshine—the creaminess makes you forget about your worries and your diet for the day. Sour cream peach pie was my dad's favorite (and it's mine too). I had to bake two pies so there would be enough for the both of us.

Dad arrived at the house with a loaf of his homemade banana bread in hand. He decorated the banana bread with red, white and blue icing for the occasion. It said, "USA."

I said hello, gave Dad a kiss on the cheek, and admired his bread.

"Nice bread, Dad. Cute! It says, 'USA!'"

"Yes! Thanks, hon," he smiled. He put the bread down on the counter and went to greet the in-laws in the backyard. Before I knew it, he left my house, and drove away from my 3rd of July party. He left the banana bread sitting on the counter.

I wasn't sure what had happened. Maybe he wasn't feeling well. I felt shocked and confused, and panic began to rise in my neck. Whether or not he felt good, I wanted him at the party. I needed him at that party. He didn't know it, but the whole party was just for him. I spent so much time and energy trying to make him happy that day. And he was going to be happy, dang it.

With that attitude, I grabbed the banana bread off the counter and placed it in the passenger seat of my car. As I drove the few blocks to his apartment, scenarios ran through my head. What had gone wrong? Why did he leave the party? I suspected he didn't want to be at the party for some reason.

I tried to maintain curiosity and concern, but my fists wrapped tight around the steering wheel as I drove. My heart pounded in my chest, my jaw clenched tight, and I could feel heat rising in my head.

When I arrived, I grabbed the banana bread and walked to Dad's door. I knocked. I let myself in. I found him piddling around.

"Dad, what's going on? Why did you leave the party? Are you not feeling well?"

"No sweetie. That's not it."

"What is it then? Did something happen?"

"No, I—"

"Tell me what's happening."

"I'm just not going."

"I baked two peach pies, Dad. A whole pie for you! Come back to the party."

"It's just that . . . It's just my dog isn't allowed at your house, but Jeff's mom and dad get to bring their dogs."

"Dad, you know why your dog isn't allowed at my house. She poops on my carpet."

I tried to hold on to reason, but my blood was at a full, rolling boil. My arms and legs twitched.

I tried to calm myself—earlier in the day, I swigged a few glasses of red wine to calm my nerves while making the peach pies, but I was at the end of my rope. My whole body shook with rage. Hot blood rushed into my face.

I screamed. Fully out of control, I hurled hurtful words across the room. I needed my words and my screaming to have some sort of effect, like Dad would yell back, or apologize, or cry, or something. He didn't.

The banana bread was at hand. I grabbed the loaf, ripped it in two, and lobbed the pieces at him. One, two.

I screamed a few more words.

"F*** you, Dad!"

My voice reverberated off the walls. Standing there in silence, I looked at Dad, looked at the mess I made, and then as quickly as I had arrived, I fled. I left his apartment and drove back home. My body shook.

Arriving back home, I parked and gripped the steering wheel. I took a few quick breaths. I relieved my grip and went inside.

"Where's your dad?" my friends and family asked.

"He's not coming. I actually threw banana bread at him."

"You threw bread at him?"

"Yes, the banana bread he made, I threw it at him. He got icing on his face."

I forced myself to laugh. I forced myself to smile. I grabbed another glass of wine. I tried to appear relaxed, but the situation wasn't funny, and I was not relaxed.

When you lose your temper, you don't feel like yourself. I'm a good person. I'm a kind mom. I'm friendly and thoughtful. But when I lost my temper, I was out of control. I wasn't myself. Or maybe I was myself, just a very raw, very hurt, very angry part of myself . . .

I tried to figure out what happened. For a few days, I re-played the party and the fight with Dad in my head. What triggered me? Was it the sour cream peach pie? Mom used to make it when I was little. She died when I was twenty-six. Perhaps it was the sight of the hot, bubbling juices spilling out over the sides of the piecrust that triggered some old grief and my subsequent rage. Or perhaps it was the party itself.

When I planned the party, I felt so stressed out, wanting it to be perfect, so Dad wouldn't feel left out—so he'd get a good taste of family and the kids and some sparklers on our American holiday. And I also kept the secret from him that he wasn't invited to come to the other party, the one happening on the 4th of July. I made my life so complicated, juggling so many balls trying to make everyone happy—especially Dad.

Eventually I realized that taking Dad's happiness into my own hands wasn't a good idea. The whole reason I'd planned the 3rd of July party was, admittedly, a bit nutty.

Then I remembered. The year before, there was a different kind of incident. I was sitting down to watch the fireworks on the 4th of July with the family in Austin, Texas. Dad, chronically ill, was in the hospital in a coma in Santa Fe, New Mexico. While the fireworks burst in the sky, I sat on a long-distance phone call with a doctor making life and death decisions for Dad—decisions he wasn't conscious enough to make.

"We need to give your Dad blood and we need your permission."

"Is that your recommendation?"

"Yes, without the blood, he'll die."

"Ok, he wants to live. So give him the blood."

Those kinds of decisions and those types of phone calls were not unusual for me as Dad's caregiver, but that one, when he was in a coma, was especially heavy.

Those decisions were my job. They had been assigned to me by everyone—Dad, our family, and even Mom before she died. I had all his legal paperwork with my name on it sitting on my desk that allowed me to make such decisions.

So, the 4th of July holiday (now a year later, after deciding to save his life and give Dad a blood transfusion) had stressed me out. Memories are funny that way. Sometimes they sneak up on you. Even when you don't know they're there. Some memories live in your bones.

A few days after I threw banana bread at him, Dad called and texted.

"Jenny, we need to talk about this."

"Jenny, we need to figure this out."

"Please call me. We need to talk about what happened."

I ignored him. I wasn't ready to talk yet. He called and texted again and again. I didn't know it yet but he was trying to get a hold of me because he had been contacted by Adult Protective Services.

If you don't know, Adult Protective Services is like Child Protective Services (also known as CPS). If you know an adult or a child in an abusive situation in the States, you're required to report it by law. These are the folks you report to and then they investigate.

Someone reported that I punched my dad.

Dad, frail from liver failure, looked 102, even though he was only seventy years old. When I threw the banana bread at him, it bounced off his chest and hit him on the cheek. For most people, it wouldn't have left anything behind but some icing (and Dad did have some of that red, white, and blue icing on his face when I walked out the door), but with Dad, the day after I threw the bread, it looked like someone had punched him. His chronically sick body was so fragile there were red marks on his face like lots of little bruises.

There's a lot of fear around Child Protective Services and Adult Protective Services, but they do good things. They try to be helpful in hard situations. I kept telling myself, "They just want to be helpful." But for days, I felt terrified. Thoughts flooded my brain as my heart raced, "What would happen? Would I lose my kids? Would I have a police record? Would this ruin my life? Would I be arrested? And, after all I'd done for him!"

Mary from Adult Protective Services went to Dad's apartment to interview him about the incident. Then she came to my house and interviewed me. We sat on my couch. She sat with an open notebook that had notes from my case. As we talked, I rubbed my hands together to keep them from shaking.

Midway through the interview I told the story about our fight. I swallowed and said, "Yes, I threw the banana bread at him." I swallowed again.

She paused, looked down at her notes and stifled a giggle.

"Was it in a tin or something?" she asked.

"No, just the bread, ma'am."

Mary closed her book. That was the end of the investigation. I didn't go to jail—at least not the kind with bars. Part of me was relieved that I didn't get in deep trouble, but I still felt trapped. I was in a prison of my own making. I thought, "How could I go on like this?" Juggling so many balls, worried about the next one that would drop, angry that I was this crazy juggler in the first place. "How did I get here? How can I get out?"

Mary said, "It's stressful to be a caregiver. What kind of support are you getting?"

"I'm seeing a counselor, but I take care of so many things for Dad, and I have my own family and kids to take care of too. It's stressing me out."

"Is there anything you can give up? Maybe you don't need to do all the things you do for your dad."

"Yes, I realize now I need to give up some things. Once a month when I sit down to take care of Dad's finances,

I freak out. He's just not good with money, and he likes to overspend. That's the first thing I'm going to let Dad figure out. I can't be a part of his finances anymore."

"Yes. Keep seeing your counselor and start there." Mary closed her notebook and left.

The day I threw banana bread, I saw red. Anger coursed through my veins. I let it take over. Anger will do that if you let it. Since then, I've learned a lot about anger.

Growing up, anger was scary. When I was a kid and Dad became angry, he yelled. His face turned red, and a wild look entered his eyes. He wasn't himself. Sometimes he spanked me, or even hit me in the rear end with his boot. As a kid, I learned anger meant you were out of control, upset, yelling.

That's what I thought anger was . . . but it's not.

Anger's a very powerful—and very common—emotion. All people feel anger.

We often feel it when we feel hurt or see someone being hurt. Like, "She shouldn't be treating me that way (that hurts me)," or, "They shouldn't be doing that to them (that hurts them)." When that happens, we often respond to hurt with hurt by threatening the person we see as hurtful. We also feel anger when we feel unsafe, like our kid nearly misses our eye with his elbow. In general, we feel anger when we wish things were different. We wish we felt loved, we wish others were always being loving towards others, and we always want to feel safe.

Here's something else I've learned about anger: Being angry does not have to mean being upset. Angry and upset are not the same thing.

Now when I get angry, I notice. And I use all that powerful energy to be helpful. Sometimes being helpful looks like simply noticing my anger and calming down: I take a lot of deep breaths, go on a walk, go out with my friends, or call my sister. Sometimes being helpful looks like taking action to help the situation: I see what I can do to make a situation safer, or more kind and loving, so the hurt turns into love and support.

Once you get out from under the control of anger, then you get to control it. You get to choose: Will I be hurtful or helpful?

Whatever you do, if you're hurtful, you know you can be powerfully hurtful. You can bring up all the old hurts and make everyone feel hurt, too. There was a part of me that used to like doing that, making everyone feel hurt. It seems strange to me as I write this, reading that last sentence in print, but it's true. I felt powerful the way I used to be able to hurt people, to make my husband yell, or to make my kids cry. As best I can, now I choose not to be hurtful anymore. Instead, I choose to be helpful.

If you choose to be helpful, you'll eventually find you have the energy to move mountains, to make a difference, to do good for your own life and for the lives of others. You can make your home and neighborhood a safer and loving place for all of you. It may be hard to believe, but you can do real good using the energy from anger (I'll share examples later).

I love Post-It™ notes. I call them "sticky notes." I use them all the time. So as a tool, I'll make suggestions for you throughout the book to use sticky notes as reminders for these ideas. Leave them up until you've mastered the idea, until the idea is no longer new, or it's just simply a part of your everyday life. Leave it up until the sticky note "sticks."

Here's your sticky note for this chapter:

Anger is powerful.

I can be helpful or hurtful with it.

Seriously . . . write this down. Put it on the fridge or on a mirror. This isn't something you'll learn overnight. It's going to take time and a few more tools in your toolbox before the idea sticks (so keep reading!).

Chapter 2
Tardy in the Morning

For most moms, the morning routine is well . . . a THING. We turn the house upside down looking for the lost shoe. Someone makes a mess in the bathroom. Someone breaks a glass. The dog pees on the floor. Breakfast ends up being a Pop Tart in the car, and on the way to school, we realize someone left homework on the table. We're driving like a maniac in the meantime, trying to get Brother to stop hitting Sister in the back seat. While yelling at Brother, we grab the brush in the coffee holder to brush our own hair so it looks like we didn't just roll out of bed.

I've broken this whole thing down to blame one item for our messy mornings—the clock.

We've given the clock a lot of power, haven't we? I wake up in the morning at 6:30 a.m. (Okay, not really. I hit snooze and then get out of bed at 6:45.) I know the tardy bell will ring at my kids' school at 8:00 a.m. I don't know why, but the tardy bell scares me.

Maybe it's the sound of the middle school bell ringing in my ears over and over again, day after day—that memory of me trying to get to my locker and back to class on time. The bell was scary with the looming threat of a dreaded trip to the middle school office for a tardy slip, my teacher giving me a disapproving stare as I walk late into class, and all the other students sitting and looking at me quietly, grateful it's not them holding the tardy slip.

The sound of that bell still rules so many households in the morning. The crack of dawn race against the clock used to stress me out so badly I yelled every morning. I yelled about the lost shoe. I yelled about the dog. I yelled about the kid having to go to the bathroom as we walked about the door. On the way to school, I yelled about the traffic. I yelled about the hitting. I yelled about the yelling! That clock and that bell were ruling my life!

One morning, we ran late as usual. I had experimented with different wake up times. It didn't matter if we had more time or less time. The time always seemed to slip by too fast. If we had more time, more things came up that had to get done. More messes, more lost shoes, more trips to the bathroom . . .

That morning, my daughter's shoes weren't on yet, but it was TIME to leave the house. She wasn't ready, so she threw herself on the floor and had a tantrum. Feeling the weight of the clock, I picked her up, myself a screaming crazy mama, and put her in the car seat. Both of us shrieking, I held her bucking body down, legs and arms flying everywhere, and buckled her seatbelt.

"EVA, HOLD STILL DAMMIT!"

A neighbor came out of their house. "Is everything ok, Jen?" I heard from behind.

I felt my cheeks turn red. A lump formed in my throat. I turned to her, "No, everything's ok, just, um, trying to get to school, you know." I forced a laugh.

"Okay," the neighbor hesitated.

My daughter continued to scream. I quickly shut the van door and got in the driver's seat. We drove away from my neighbor, still watching us from her drive way as I sped out of the neighborhood.

Then my daughter began kicking the back of my seat. Like really kicking. It felt like someone was punching me in the back.

I pulled over.

"Pulling over" is pretty much the scariest threat a kid can experience when they have a mom or a dad who loses it in the car. When my dad used to pull over, I knew I would get a spanking, and there was no place to run! No place to hide!

I warned my daughter that she better stop kicking the seat. Then I yelled.

"STOP KICKING THE SEAT! STOP IT! STOPPIT!"

I opened my door, and got out of the van. I opened her door, pulled her out of the car seat, spanked her, and put her back in the seat.

She cried quietly. She stopped kicking the seat.

As I got back in my seat, I tried to tell myself that I was doing my job, "It's not ok to kick the seat. My daughter needs discipline." But the lump in my throat persisted. I tried hard to swallow it down. My jaw clenched and I gripped the steering wheel with tight fists like I had so many times before. I took a breath.

I did feel some release because I had done my job for the morning. This was my job—to be a mom, to get the kids to school, to teach them what's right and what's wrong. Did I love this? No, not really. There was a part of me that hated this job, and I hated myself.

This was the routine, and since I had released my anger for the morning, I could relax. We all could relax now. It was part of our whole family's routine. We were all used to the way I lost it daily.

As much as we might say we hate the morning routine or the tardy bell, there is a sort of excitement from urgency. We get a rush from it. When you lose your temper, you get a literal rush of adrenaline and other chemicals in the body and brain.

As much as we might feel guilty about yelling, there's a small part of us that likes it. Some of us feel better afterward. We've gotten our hot temper "hit" for the day. Now we can breathe.

The only problem is, alongside this darker part of me, I had a healthy conscience telling me all this yelling wasn't a good thing.

I lay awake at night replaying those moments in my head. Feeling the guilt still lodged in my heart, I would tell myself, "That'll be the last time," over and over. "Today's the last time I lose my temper. It won't happen again. I won't yell like that at the kids ever again." But I knew that wouldn't be the last time. In fact, it would probably happen again tomorrow.

Yelling → Shame → Guilt

Yelling → Shame → Guilt

I was trapped.

Are you trapped too?

Here's a secret to escape the trap: Yelling is a habit you can break. It's a habit I learned from my Dad, and he learned it from his Dad. I broke the habit with mentors, tools, and practice. All of the things I'm sharing with you in this book can help you break the habit, too.

That guilt you feel can give you the energy to take responsibility and do something new. Here's a thought about habits that can help you in your first steps:

For a moment, let's think about cigarette smoking. It's a habit that's easy to use as an example. People are addicted to the nicotine, but they've also made smoking a routine, like maybe a cigarette in the morning or right before bed. Or maybe there are certain people with whom they normally smoke, so just being around them triggers their cravings.

It's the same with yelling. We're addicted to the adrenaline rush of it. Like clockwork, I used to lose my temper with the kids in the morning before school, especially with my daughter. And there were certain people who were used to it—my kids and husband. They never said anything. It was just the way I was "disciplining" or "raising" the kids.

Sadly, each of them received a rush of adrenaline, too. When I yelled, it was scary. Even though they didn't like it, their bodies were used to responding to it, just like mine was.

Breaking the habit of yelling is multi-dimensional. It's about the mind and the body. It's about learning how to stay calm physically. It's also about creating new routines with the whole family. It involves new habits like getting help and learning how to feel feelings in healthy ways. You also need new methods that work for disciplining the kids (more on all that later).

But for now, let's keep it simple. Here's your sticky note for this chapter:

Yelling is a habit you can break.

Take a moment and write this down on a sticky note. Put it on a book you read daily or your bathroom mirror or perhaps at your seat at the dining table. When you read it, hear it in your own voice. Tell yourself you can break this habit. Hear me telling you too, as your cheerleader, "You can break this habit mama! I've done it, and you can too." Thinking of yelling as a habit is the first place to begin, because our thoughts lead to actions.

Finally, let me tell you another tidbit to inspire you about the morning routine. The tardy bell doesn't stress me out anymore. If we're late, we're late. But friend, we're not late. In fact, because we're all usually pretty calm in the morning, we have enough time to do everything we need to do . . . and then some. We find shoes quicker, we solve problems with ease (most of the time), and everybody gets to go to the bathroom. If I do feel that clock weighing on my shoulders, I take a deep breath and lie down on the couch. It sounds funny, but it's true. I lie down because *my* calm

19

matters. It helps time slow down, and it helps us get out the door on time.

Chapter 3

Breaking the Silence

I went to a life-coaching group on a Friday night. The topic was "Strengthen Your Relationships." Each person who showed up was given the opportunity to choose something to work on.

I chose to work on beating myself up. As in, I wanted to stop doing that. Like I said, I beat myself up a lot, mostly at night as I drifted off to sleep, going over all my mistakes from the day. I made myself miserable thinking about how mean I had been to the kids. Sometimes, to add to my misery, I'd remember mistakes from my past too, regrets from my days as a young adult, and even regrets from my childhood, like the time I stole a piece of fashion jewelry out of my best friend Lisa's doll house. I was 5 years old. For decades, I hated myself for doing that.

So at the life-coaching group, when it was my turn, I stood up as I was told to do. Mike, the life coach, then told me to talk about what I wanted to work on. I did.

"I want to work on beating myself up."

"What do you mean?"

"I beat myself up."

"What does that mean?"

"I beat myself up in my head. I think about mistakes I've made. I think about all the times I've screwed up. All the time."

"Jeanette, look around at the group, pick one person to speak to and tell them what you want to work on."

I followed his directions precisely, as all good perfectionists do. I picked one person and I said, "I want to stop beating myself up."

Mike watched me and then took a long pause. He observed, "Jeanette, you're so good."

"What?" I was confused.

"Jeanette, you're good. A good person. I can't see why you beat yourself up."

I felt a lump in my throat. Heat in my face. Guilt crept up my spine.

"You don't know me... I'm not as good as you think."

"What then? Why do you beat yourself up? Give us an example."

I thought for a long time. I scrolled through the never-ending list in my head of all the things I felt guilty about.

"I yell at my kids," I said quietly. I said it so quietly Mike didn't hear me. I swallowed hard. It was difficult saying it the first time.

"Say that again?"

I cleared my throat, "I yell at my kids. I scream at them. I screamed at my little girl yesterday."

I had talked about yelling at the kids with my friends, but that was the first time I had ever told a professional who could help me stop the yelling.

"Tell us what happened. Where were you? Describe it for us. I'm having a hard time imagining you yelling."

I was skilled at hiding my rage. I could bottle it up in public in order to maintain the appearance of having everything under control. My parents taught me how to hide the tough stuff well.

Embarrassed as I was, I felt determined to convince Mike I was a yeller. I wanted him to see me—the real me. Part of me knew that was the only way I could get help. So, I told Mike about the day before.

"We took a walk around the block yesterday. The kids wanted to go one way down the block, and I wanted to go the other. After arguing with me over and over, I screamed at them to get my way."

Mike was amazed and quietly pondered, "How could such a good, loving mom like you yell like that?"

He was curious. He was also genuinely dumbfounded. Lovingly, he asked, "Why did you yell? Try to put yourself back in that moment."

Standing in front of the group, resisting the urge to run out of the room, I closed my eyes and tried to put myself back in that place.

"I don't know. I, I . . . just wanted my kids to . . . follow directions . . . They weren't listening to me . . . "

Mike tried to unravel it, to chip away at it. He had never met a mom like me, at least not a mom who admitted the yelling, so he didn't get very far. But that first moment, that simple confession that I yell at my kids, was enough to start my transformation.

Here's what I've discovered: The moms I meet who yell at their kids rarely talk about it. They don't even have a word for it.

So that's where you begin. You find a word for it. You name it. You tell someone; you tell several people, "I'm a yeller, and I want to stop yelling."

Tell your kids, tell your husband.

The next day after the life coaching group, I talked to my kids about it. I called it the Anger Bug. I said I got the bug from my dad. He got it from his dad, and I didn't want the Anger Bug anymore. I wanted to squish it. To kill it. That was the best I could do, the best way I could describe what was going on. I was using words like a toddler, but that's where I was—I was just learning to walk and talk around learning to feel my feelings. I had to start somewhere.

So who are your support people? I'm not talking about just your normal support people. It's likely your normal support people support your yelling habit. They might think this whole thing is silly. Or unnecessary. They might think yelling is just discipline, or that the kids deserve to be yelled at.

But you're different. Something inside you is telling you that you don't want to be that kind of mom anymore. I know because I've been there, and coached many parents who have been there also.

Then there's this other thing we've touched on: shame. Mama, to get help, you're gonna need to reach up through that muck you're under and say, "Hey, I need some help under here!" Shame, in some way, has been a blessing, a coping tool, a place for you to hide. There's probably a lot of sadness in that muck you're hiding under, too. But it's time to come out and wash your face—to let go of the shame and move through the sadness go, so you can move on and move up to bigger and better things for your life.

My yelling used to be kind of secret. I didn't want the neighbors to know. I used to yell in my house, but I didn't yell in public. There was a part of me that knew it was wrong. I was embarrassed and afraid. Embarrassed that I didn't know how to handle my kids, and afraid of being judged.

You might be thinking that you can do this all by yourself. That's what you've been taught, right? In my family, I was taught to pull myself up by my own bootstraps. It would have looked like airing our dirty laundry to go outside the family. In my childhood house, we stuffed our dirty messes into the nearest drawer or under the couch to hide them. Others weren't allowed to see our imperfections, and they weren't asked for help, because that would have been an admission of weakness, of problems. Problems? No, not us.

I'm guessing you might be from a family like mine, and if you are, mama, you've been so strong; you can handle anything. You've handled so many things, but this one thing, this yelling thing, is going to take more than just you, more than your family, to help you. It took a lot of practice for me to share the hard things in my life. Little by little, I took out a little problem, a dirty little sock from under the old "family" couch, and eventually, as I experienced healing, I heaped loads and loads of dirty laundry on the floor, asking family, experts, and friends to help me wash.

A lot of folks have probably leaned on you over the years, and now it's your turn. So I ask, (and this is your sticky note):

Who will I tell?

I'm a yeller and I want to stop yelling.

Start with your kids. Tell your dog. (Do you yell at them too?) Tell your husband. Ask for their support. Tell them you're learning how to be the mom you want to be—a kind, patient mom who is in control.

28

Chapter 4
The Stages of Learning

Right now if you're saying, "I'm a yeller and I want to stop yelling," you're in the most painful stage of learning. I've seen it in the face of many moms when they first meet me at networking events. In that one quick moment while we're shaking hands and introducing ourselves, they learn they don't have to yell anymore, that maybe they didn't have to yell all along. They learn they can be a strong, respected mom and still be kind, but they don't know how to do it yet.

I've seen lots of moms cry. I've even seen moms get angry with me. "Oh, everyone yells at their kids. I yell at mine every day!" said one mom as her cheeks turned red and tears welled up in her eyes. After a long pause, she quietly said, "So how do you do it? How do you stop yelling?"

It's frustrating when you first realize there's something you don't know, and all of a sudden you want to know everything about it. You want to stop yelling, like yesterday. You want to go back in time and have all the re-dos. You want to hide under the couch or go yell some more. You want to forget you ever met me or picked up this book. It's such a painful place, and I'm sorry for the pain.

But please hear me when I tell you, "This is part of the process." The pain you feel is part of the second stage of learning, and it won't last forever. Through this process, you'll learn to be gentle on your kids—and yourself too. It's just going to take time. For now, move through the embarrassment. It's going to be okay. Let those sad and mad feelings come up and out. Cry to a friend. Punch a pillow. Call your counselor. Yell at me into the air.

In the first stage of learning, you don't know what you don't know. You yell at your kids, and it's normal because that's what you were taught by your parents. You're doing the best you can disciplining your kids and raising them with traditional methods of punishments, rewards, threats, and consequences.

In the second stage of learning (this is the most painful part), you realize there's something you don't know, and you want to learn it. (This might be where you are right now.)

In the third stage of learning, you've learned some new things and you're practicing. As you read this book, you'll learn things you can do and words you can say so you can formulate a new plan for disciplining your kids. In the third stage, you might accidentally slip back into the old ways, such as accidentally yelling again. It takes concentration to do things the new way, but it gets easier day-by-day.

In the fourth stage of learning, you don't have to think about it anymore. Your new ways come easily. You have a whole new set of tools, and the old tools are just that—old tools. You don't need them anymore. That's when you take your sticky notes down one-by-one, because you don't need the reminders. Your new ways have finally "stuck." (On my good days, I'm in the fourth stage of learning. I haven't yelled like my old self in over a year now—2018 was the last time.)

There's this idea that's popular in schools and workplaces right now called the "growth mindset." (Carol Dweck was one of the originators.)[1] Even though it may feel painful, try to have a growth mindset. Having a growth mindset means knowing the power of "yet." When you were little, you didn't know how to read "yet," but you learned.

I coached a dad yesterday who said, "I don't have patience for my three-year-old." (Yes, I've helped dads too.)

I replied, "You don't have the patience—yet."

He took a deep breath and nodded, "Yes."

The pain of embarrassment is just the second stage of learning, and you are learning (congratulations on getting this far!). With time, the embarrassment will fade.

This is the growth mindset, the power of "yet." You don't know what you want to know *yet*, but you will. Here's your sticky note:

I'm in the second stage of learning.

It's painful not knowing, but I will learn.

Chapter 5

Screaming Over Spilt Bubbles

I teach classes. I taught a class about anger at a yoga studio. You might not think there are angry people at a yoga studio, but there are angry people everywhere. I asked them to think of a time they felt annoyed.

One woman said, "When another driver pulls out in front of me, it drives me crazy."

A man offered, "When my sister tries to tell me and my wife what to do, I just want to strangle her."

I asked them to describe the physical feeling in their bodies when they're annoyed. Those in the group responded:

"I feel tightness in my neck and shoulders."

"I feel heat at the top of my head."

"I feel tightness in my chest, like I can't breathe."

"My jaw's tight."

"My stomach feels upset."

I nodded as they shared. I've heard this list of bodily sensations over and over. Usually, this is what people feel in their bodies when they're annoyed. This is what I call "The Button."

Surprisingly, most people all over the world experience The Button in the same way.[1] We also experience other feelings, like fear, happiness, and sadness in similar ways. For example, many people feel warmth in their chest and tingling in their bodies when they feel very happy or when they feel loved.

When I coach moms who lose their temper, I ask them, "Where do you feel it in your body right before you lose it? What does it feel like?"

They always say, "I've never thought about that before."

This is what I want you to think about now: What does your Button feel like? When you're annoyed, when you're about to yell, what does it feel like in your body? Do you agree with the list of sensations above, or are your sensations different?

Noticing how your Button feels will help you stop yelling because you can catch yourself. Realize, you won't catch yourself every time at first. This takes practice. But you'll get better at it.

I want to share with you the story about the day I screamed over spilt bubbles. It was another rock bottom button-pushing moment for me.

I had one of those big containers of bubbles—the gigantic ones from Wal-Mart they sell for summertime fun. The kids and I often hung out in the backyard to pass our summer days, and this day was like every other day. We chose an outdoor activity—blowing bubbles. The kids and I held smaller containers of bubbles, which I refilled with the large container. I placed the large container in the middle of the table, out of reach from the toddlers (or so I thought). I went inside for a moment to change a diaper.

When I came back outside, my little girl stood grinning, holding the giant container of bubbles in her hands. Sneaky little girl, she had climbed up on the table and retrieved it while I was gone

I watched with frustration as she giggled and then dumped the bubbles out. Every last drop on the lawn. No biggie normally. One of those containers of bubbles probably runs about $3. And I didn't have a mess to clean up—it was just seeping into the grass.

But that day, for whatever reason, I was at the end of my rope. Maybe I was tired from the night before. Maybe the tasks of the day were looming and, in my fatigue, seemingly difficult. As for my plan of putting the big bubble container out of reach, it had failed. My Button was pushed. My breathing became shallow and my jaw clenched while my fingers curled into fists. I screamed. Eva screamed. I picked her up and spanked her. My hand made a muffled smacking sound as it made contact with her diaper. I put her in "time out" in a corner of the backyard.

"TIME OUT!" I yelled.

"Bubbles, mama!" she cried.

"There are no more bubbles! You dumped them all out!" I held the bubble container over her head to show her it was empty, but it wasn't entirely empty, and some of the bubble mixture trickled out onto her hair.

As I saw the goop in her hair, blood rushed out of my face, and my breath caught in my throat. I stomped my foot and looked away. "Dammit," I said through gritted teeth.

My little girl reached up, touched her hair, looked at her hand, and sadly whispered, "Bubbles." She started crying. She didn't like having bubbles in her hair, so I took her to the sink and washed her off. This could have been a warm, loving bath. It wasn't. The water was cold, and so was I. I set her on the floor, used a dishtowel to wipe the water from her head, and walked away, feeling numb and stiff, like a robot. I needed a "mommy time out."

Time slowed down for the rest of the day. Toddlers need a lot from their mommies, and I moved like molasses, deliberate with every move, doing my best to ignore the raging storm of confusion, regret, rage, and sadness knocking away in my chest. As I made snacks and did the dishes, I went through the motions, but I wasn't present. My mind escaped to a far off place—far from the kids, far from the dishes, and far from myself.

That night in bed, I made plans for the next day. We would do bubbles again. I needed a redo. Big time. "Tomorrow, we'll play with bubbles, and she'll probably dump them out again. Tomorrow, I'll give her a kiss instead."

So we did play with bubbles again. The next morning, we got out our small containers of bubbles, the ones we had left. I stood and watched my daughter smile at me as she held her container high in the air. Then she took the container and poured the bubbles out onto the lawn. She watched them seep into the ground. She paused and looked up at me. I paused, too, and took a breath. This was my moment.

I walked over to her and said, "I love you, sweetheart. I know I yelled about the bubbles yesterday, but I don't want to do that anymore. I'm trying to do better, sweetie." I gave her a kiss on the cheek.

We went through the rest of the day as normal. I thought that was the end of the bubble incident, but it wasn't. That evening, as I tucked her into bed, little Eva said, "Dump bubbles out." She didn't have a lot of words as a toddler yet, so she said again, "Dump bubbles out." I heard her, and I understood that with those three little words, she was saying a lifetime of things.

"Mama, why did you dump the bubbles on my head? I didn't like that. Mama, I'm sad that you got so mad. Mama, why do you yell? Mama, I don't like it when you yell. Mama, aren't we supposed to have fun? Don't you love me?" I knew those were words she would say if she could. Her little brain was confused. Her soul was hurt.

I told her, "Yes, sweetie, you dumped the bubbles out yesterday, and I yelled. I lost it. And I'm so sorry about the bubbles on your head. Today, you dumped the bubbles out again, and this time, I didn't yell. Instead, I gave you a kiss. I'm trying to do better baby. I'm sorry. I love you." I kissed her goodnight.

I walked out of the room biting my lip and fell asleep with a stiff neck, holding my eyes shut tight to prevent the tears from spilling.

The very next night as I tucked her into bed, little Eva's voice called out again, "Dump bubbles out."

So I told her again, "Yes, honey. You dumped the bubbles out, and I lost it. I'm sorry about that. I'm trying to stop doing that. Please forgive me. I love you."

She went off to sleep.

The next night, three days after the bubble incident, my husband Jeff came in to tell me that Eva was ready for bed. He said, "She keeps talking about bubbles. She wants to play with bubbles or something, but I told her it's time for bed." He didn't understand what she was saying because she couldn't form those complex sentences yet.

My cheeks flushed, and with a lump in my throat I looked down and said, "Oh yes, she just . . . she just . . . wants to play with bubbles." I didn't have the courage to tell Jeff what had happened. I rushed out of the room and knelt down at Eva's side.

"Mama, dump bubbles out."

"I know, sweetie, I know. I know. I'm so sorry. I'm sorry, baby. I love you. I love you so much. I'm trying to do better."

"Dump bubbles out."

"I know, sweetie. Remember the second day, when you dumped out the bubbles, and I didn't get mad? I told you, 'I love you' and gave you a kiss. I'm trying to do better." I kissed her goodnight and sat with her in the dark, listening to her breathe. I sat there a long time and waited until she breathed the long sigh, the one that told me she was asleep.

Then, the next night at bedtime, she said again, "Dump bubbles out." And the next night and the next. After a week, I started counting the nights she said, "Dump bubbles out."

For twenty-one nights, my daughter's sweet little voice asked me, asked the universe, asked God, "Dump bubbles out?"

And all I could say was, "I'm sorry, honey. I love you. I'll try not to do that again."

Dear mama, I know you have a story like this, a story when you threw a cup, a story when you yelled, a story when you just couldn't take it anymore, and all of your buttons were pushed, and you lost it. And I want to tell you: "Breathe. It's okay. I've been there too. Now you're making a choice. You want to stop doing that, and I want you to stop doing it, too (I'm praying for you)."

So here's your sticky note for today. It's to develop awareness, so you can get better and better and stop it— yelling, screaming, threatening, or criticizing—before it happens. It's your Button. What does it feel like?

Write on your sticky note:

Where do I feel my anger in my body?

What does it feel like?

Take notes. Feel what it feels like. Do you feel it in your neck? Head? Jaw? Shoulders? Stomach? Hips? Chest? Fists? Does it feel tight? Hot?

Become fully aware of it. The next time you feel those feelings in your body, you can take a pause and do something else. What else can you do? Read the next chapter to find out.

Side note: Have you noticed the pattern that I usually lost my temper with my little girl? In families, it's usually one kid who triggers the yelling. It's usually the kid we think has problems. We used to think my little girl had big problems, and she did (learning how to cope with stress in healthy ways just like her mama was the main problem), but I needed to address my own behavior first. Do you have one kid who triggers you?

Chapter 6

Mama Lions Yawn

I grew up watching nature documentaries on PBS. Two images stick out in my mind. First, is the image of lions chasing their prey—a small gazelle. It's intense, wondering if they'll catch their lunch or not, and I usually felt relieved if the gazelle got away.

The second image from those documentaries I remember is of lions lazing around. They looked so relaxed in the tall grass. Blinking long blinks, half napping as their cubs nipped at their paws. They snuggled up with each other, had fun, and lay happily in the sun.

So how do they do that? How do lions gather all that energy to hunt their lunch and then go and relax so easily? One thing they do is yawn. I've seen my little dog do it, too. After she's had a stressful moment, or even if I pet her on a stressful day, my little dog Minnie yawns. Sometimes, she gives her head or her whole body a shake. Cats do it, too.

Lions and our cats and dogs know how to release that stressful energy, and we can learn from them. One of the keys is to observe how animals work in packs. Lions hunt together. If one is stressed out, working hard to catch her lunch, they all are. The stress is contagious, and that's a blessing because it helps them work together. The same thing happens to humans. Stress is contagious. If a neighbor comes over and there's an emergency, their energy passes on to me, and it puts me in action to help them.

In today's culture, the way stress gets passed around isn't usually a blessing anymore. If one of my kids gets stressed out, it's just not necessary for me to get stressed out, too. Or if another driver on the road gets stressed out and pulls out in front of me, it's not helpful for me to take on his or her stress and fill myself with rage.

The good news is that calm is contagious, too. In the same way that stress can be passed around, calm can be passed around. You see this clearly in that pack of lions. When one of them yawns, the other lions yawn, too. When I was a yeller, I was passing around the stress. Now that I'm in control, I've learned to pass around the calm.

This morning, my son was stressed out because he couldn't find the ball he wanted to bring to school. He kept looking and looking. It was time to leave the house, and I felt my shoulders tense up. But I took a yawn breath and sat down, saying, "I'll be here as long as you need." In my mind, I decided it would be just fine if we got to school late.

As soon as I sat down, he paused, took a breath, and said, "Well, I guess I can just find it later after school," and we made it to school on time.

The next time you feel your Button being pushed, here's what I want you to try: Yawn. Yawn like your dog yawns. Not the prim and proper yawn where we try not to open our mouths and cover it up with our hands. Be the mama lion, ahead of your pack, proudly showing off that giant yawn. To get specific, here are some steps. I call this the "Perfect Yawn," and it helps your body and mind calm down.

The Perfect Yawn

1. If you need to, step away from a stressful situation for a moment.
2. Think about a time you felt the way you want to feel (perhaps snuggling on the couch with a blanket).
3. Relax your eyes and forehead.
4. Bring your tongue down from the roof of your mouth. (Pay attention to your tongue—if it's pressed up against the roof of your mouth, you might be feeling stressed out.)
5. Tilt your head side to side, give it a little shake, and loosen your neck muscles.
6. Bring your shoulders down from your ears.
7. Yawn with a long exhale. Open your mouth wide.
8. Open the space at the back of the throat.
9. Loosen your jaw.
10. Relax your chest and back.

11. Let your belly drop. Relax the muscles at the bottom of your ribs.

12. Relax your gluts (your butt).

13. Keep yawning.

14. Wiggle your knees, feet, and toes.

15. Massage your scalp.

16. Stretch.

17. Shake your whole body like a cat does.

18. Sigh (make noise).

19. Repeat.

20. Notice how you feel afterward.

With practice, it takes six seconds to physically calm down.[1] Yawning is an immediate body hack that says, "Calm down." When I calm down, my muscles feel more relaxed—particularly my jaw and shoulders. Sometimes, tingles run up and down my body.

You're the mama lion now. You're in control, and you want your calm to be contagious. You want your baby lions to yawn, too.

I watched a video of a human mama yawn for her tiny baby. She was changing a diaper, and the baby became frustrated, kicking her tiny feet. The mama said, "Breathe," and took a deep yawn breath close to the baby's face so the baby could see her. The baby took a big yawn breath too, and her legs calmed. Yawns are contagious for babies, too! When my babies were tiny and their legs thrashed around during a diaper change, I used one hand to change the diaper and one hand to hold the legs! Diaper wrestling. Very frustrating. And not very much fun. So here's your sticky note:

Mama lions YAWN.

Yawn, mama. Yawn those buttons away, one button at a time. It will take time and practice. Remember, it's not only you who has this habit of stress in the home. It's the whole family. Your calm will have its ripple effects, but it won't be immediate. The other folks in the house—your kids and husband—will probably be stressed out a little while longer. But hold steady. Hold your head high. You're the mama lion now, and you're in control.

Chapter 7

Crying is Like Pooping

I had a rough morning with the kids before school yesterday. I knocked on my little boy's door and saw he was playing. My lips tightened when I saw he wasn't ready, and I said, "Please get ready for school. It's time."

"Okay, Mom, geez!" he reacted.

"You can play after you're ready to go," I reminded through gritted teeth.

"I'm fine Mom, leave me alone," he said.

I left him and went to make breakfast downstairs. I called up, "Kids! Come on. Breakfast is ready."

My boy blew up, "Okay! Stop telling me what to do, Mom! I HATE YOU!"

Oh, boy. My old self would have lost it. I would have screamed back upstairs, "SHUT UP! Get down here by the time I count to three, OR ELSE. . ."

My old self would have shut down all emotions except anger. Anger was my armor, and it made me seem impenetrable on the surface. Now, after doing so much work to feel all my feelings, I've let down the armor and become vulnerable in some ways. When my son said he hated me, it hurt my feelings that day, and I felt it. Feeling hurt, I told him,

"It is absolutely not okay to speak to me that way." I breathed. I yawned. I felt heaviness in my chest. I told him, "That hurt my feelings. Please speak to me kindly."

My son whined and apologized, "Sorry, Mom."

We finished our morning. I dropped the kids off at school and went on my usual bike ride. During the ride, I let myself cry. I felt sad.

There's a give and take in emotionally intelligent relationships. On a really good day, I would have known that his response was just a reaction to my initial annoyance when I saw he wasn't getting ready. I wouldn't have taken his yelling personally. Instead, I would have asked him if he was okay and tried to have a redo for both of us.

But that day, his behavior hurt me, and it's okay that I let him see it because we are in relationship with each other. His behavior does have an impact on me sometimes. It's not good to make him feel responsible for my feelings all the time, but that day, an apology helped our relationship heal. Crying helped, too. Crying helped me honor myself and let go of my sadness.

Crying is like pooping—it's good and necessary for our health. Feeling all of our feelings is good and necessary for our health. The key is to feel our feelings in healthy ways.

All of them. Not just the feelings of sadness and anger, but fear and happiness too.

My feelings used to control me, and the outcome was often hurtful. When I felt angry, scared or sad, I would get upset. Sometimes I would yell or eat too much, or drink too much wine. Even when I felt happy, sometimes I drank too much wine, or ate too much cake. If I hadn't cried on that day my son yelled, I might have gone to the pantry and stuffed my mouth with chocolate, or later in the day, I might have yelled at the kids. Crying lets the sadness out, and if you don't let the sadness out, it comes out sideways and backwards, like yelling at the kids.

Now that I'm aware of my feelings, I choose how to respond to them. It's not that my feelings are gone or unimportant. I don't stuff my feelings down or ignore them. Actually, I've come to believe that feelings are very important. They guide me. When I get angry, I figure out who's hurt and try to help. When I'm sad, I cry. When I feel stress, I do things to address the stress, then nurture and soothe myself. When I'm happy, I dance, I smile, I laugh. When I'm scared, there's usually a problem to solve, so I work on solving the problem and get help.

All of our feelings are important. And we can learn to have healthy, helpful responses to all feelings. If you're a yeller, and you want to stop yelling, this is a big lesson to learn.

I grew up in a house where feelings weren't important. Well, my feelings weren't important. What was important was how Dad was feeling. Everyone worked to make sure he was happy. He told us what to do and we listened. We ignored our own feelings. My mother ignored herself so much that she gave up her life for him. Mom was influenced by Christian ideas around sacrifice—she thought it was godly to sacrifice herself for those she loved. Mom didn't give up her life for Dad in one dramatic moment, but over many years, ignoring herself the way an overweight nurse does. She took care of patients, working sixty-hour weeks. She took care of demanding doctors in the operating room. And at home, she took care of Dad. In the same way I had taken on my dad's happiness on the 3rd of July, she had taken on his happiness for her whole married life. Mom died early, at the age of fifty-eight doing just that, ignoring herself in an effort to be loving as she understood love to be.

After I threw the banana bread and Mary from Adult Protective Services visited my house, I knew I was following in Mom's footsteps. I was losing my life to this man. Sacrificing myself . . . and not in a good way.

It was work to get in touch with my feelings. I slowly allowed myself to feel the stress of raising kids and being a caregiver for Dad. Once I felt how stressful it was, I realized I couldn't handle all of that work by myself anymore, so I needed to make some changes and ask for help. I had to address the stress.

I needed to feel my love for Dad and at the same time, feel love for myself. I needed to understand that the best thing I could do was allow others to help him, not just me. A lot of sadness came up. I cried about Mom. I cried about Dad. I cried about lost time. I cried about yelling at my kids.

Crying is like pooping. It's the sadness that's got to come out, so you can live your best life.

To get in touch with all those feelings, feel the bodily sensations and give them a name. Here's what I mean: In previous chapters, we've talked about what anger feels like in the body (tight chest, clenched jaw, etc.). Now, think about what sadness feels like. Then, what does happiness feel like? What does it feel like when you're worried you're going to get in trouble, like when a police officer pulls you over for speeding? That's what fear feels like. What does it feel like when your cozy, safe, and relaxed?

Once you can describe the sensations in your body for various emotions, you'll want to give your feelings names. Anger, sadness, happiness, and fear are just a few, but there are many words in the English language to help us name our feelings.

To give you an idea, here is a list of words the moms in one of my workshops came up with when we talked about feeling annoyed:

Mad

Angry

Rageful

Helpless

Frustrated

Sad

Lonely

Burned out

Disappointed

Anxious

Overwhelmed

Defensive

Scared

Exhausted

Disgusted

Hurt

Defeated

Unappreciated

There are so many words to describe that one feeling we call "annoyed."

When I work with moms who lose their temper, this is one of the toughest tasks in the beginning. They don't know what their feelings feel like in their bodies, and they don't have the words to name the feelings yet. Being able to feel your feelings physically and name them with a few descriptive words will help you.

When you begin to do this, old stories usually come up. Stories about yourself, stories about your relationships, stories about your childhood. Along with those stories, a lot of feelings come up, including sadness. This is where your support system comes in. Remember the sticky note that says, "Who can I talk to?" Talk to those people you identified. Tell them your stories. Tell them your feelings, and know this: They might not be able to hear you, yet. They're not used to you loving on you in this way. They're not used to you honoring your own feelings. You might even need to reach out to someone new at this point, someone you haven't leaned on before. It might even be a counselor, or perhaps an old teacher.

*

Over time, you'll begin to see that feelings are important. When you feel them and name them, they no longer control you. After that, they can be your wisdom to guide you, to let you know when you need something, or to tell you when you need to take action. When you feel your feelings, you can make a choice about how you respond to them. So, practice making healthy responses and healthy choices around your feelings.

We're going to talk more about this later, but here are some examples of healthy responses to feelings. Dance in the kitchen when you're happy (that's what I do). Put on your favorite song and sing along. Cry when you feel sad. If it's not appropriate in the moment, make time to cry later. When you feel stress, yawn and stretch. Figure out what's stressing you out and address the problem. Then, do something healthy, like snuggle with a blanket, to soothe yourself. Stress is a feeling, too. You can handle it. Breathe when you feel angry. If you feel sad or angry, there might be problems to solve also. But first, identify your feelings.

Here's a helpful tool for when you're feeling your feelings: Don't say, "I'm angry" or "I'm stressed" or "I'm scared." Instead, say "I'm *feeling* angry" or "I'm *feeling* stressed" or "I'm *feeling* scared."

You're safe, and you can handle that feeling. Really, you can. More than that, over time, your feelings can become a blessing for you. They can point you in the right direction and give you energy to do what's helpful.

Feelings are important. All of them are. Increase your vocabulary and start using the language of feelings in your house. Here's a list to get your started (copy these onto a sticky note):

I'm feeling . . . angry, sad, happy, scared, excited, nervous, confused, guilty, defensive, determined, disappointed, overwhelmed, embarrassed, exhausted, frustrated, grateful, hopeful, hurt, jealous, lonely, loved, loving, relieved, safe, shocked, sorry, stressed, surprised.

This list of words might take two sticky notes, or if you're reading this, and you'd like a printable PDF called "Feelings for the Fridge," I made a special hidden page on my website just for you, where you can download it to print and hang somewhere visible. Go here:

jeanettehargreaves.com/feelings

By using the printable, you'll notice that some feelings are connected. For example, rage is often connected to helplessness, and overwhelmed is usually a combination of feelings. Use this reference list until naming your emotions becomes second nature to you. In my house, I knew we were getting somewhere when my kids started using these words too, "Mama, I feel frustrated, sad, and mad."

Finally, know this: Where there is anger, there is usually sadness. If you can dig down deep and find the sadness under the anger, pull it out. Crying is like pooping. It will be good for you and good for your anger, too.

This chapter is special because it has two sticky notes. The first sticky note is a list of feelings words. Here's your second sticky note:

I'm safe and I can handle this feeling.

Chapter 8

The Bad News

When you decide it's time to stop yelling, it's a process. First, I got down to yelling once a day, then once a week, then once a month. That's the tipping point. When you lose your temper just once a month, it seems shocking, and you and your family aren't used to it anymore. By that point, when it did happen, I would take a big step back, apologize, and work on whatever was stressing me out. There was one day like that when I lost it. It was a morning when I read the news first thing (something I rarely do).

I'm editing this manuscript during our shelter-in-place order for COVID-19. Originally, this was a long chapter about my experiences in the news and how it tends to stress us out. But I decided to re-write it in light of current circumstances.

I was a young news producer for nine years. Hans Rosling said, "Forming your worldview by relying on the media would be like forming your view about me by looking only at a picture of my foot. Sure my foot is part of me, but it's a pretty ugly part."[1] But the news doesn't have to be this way. The news is responsive to us. It's commercial. News producers produce news that we want to see. They produce news according to our views and clicks. Sadly, we tend to want to see tragedy.

One day, six years after leaving my career in the news, I walked through an airport where they stream the news on big screens everywhere. It was 2007, and an image of Brittany Spears with a shaved head appeared on every screen. My heart broke for her. She looked like she was having a rough moment, in need of some tender love and care. Instead, the news used her distress for ratings.

There's a movement in journalism called solutions-based journalism. They teach journalists to focus on solutions to problems. You can tell a solutions-based article because the solution presents in the headline, and the bulk of the story covers the solution's effectiveness. During the COVID-19 event, the solutions-based articles say that sheltering in place works, so that's what my family is doing. I don't click on articles that are not solutions-based, and I largely avoid the news otherwise.

If I had a solutions-based headline for Part I of this book it would be, "Yelling is a habit that can be broken." This news is such good news to me, I've written this book, and I've created a business around it, teaching everyone who's ready to break the habit. The solutions for yelling include getting help for the habit, and practicing new habits.

One new habit you can adopt is a way to engage with and think about the news. I'm suggesting this because it might help to lower some of the ongoing stress you feel. The news isn't just what's happening "out there" in the world; it's also what's happening in your neighborhood and in your house. And if we're worried about the world, we have the opportunity to make the world a better place simply by starting at home—by learning how to stop yelling at our kids.

During this shelter-in-place, I know a single woman who is miserable. She found a lot of news articles about how this time is tough for single people. Another single woman I know is motivated. She found articles about how this is an exciting time for single people, an opportunity to learn and grow. The two women are having entirely different experiences simply based on the news they choose to interact with and how they respond to it. It's like that old Bible verse, "Knock and the door will be opened to you."[2]

To me, that Bible verse teaches focus. Your focus matters. Focus on tragedy, and you get tragedy. Focus on solutions, and you get solutions. Focus on the good, and you see and experience more good. In a way, we're all news producers. We produce the news in our own lives. So here's your sticky note:

What is the good news in my life?

Focus on the good. Be your own news producer. Also, find other people, other types of "news producers," who produce stories of hope instead of fear, who talk about solutions instead of blame. Together, we can and will make the world a better place.

Chapter 9

Throwing Away Mom's Shoes

Now back to the banana bread. On the week I threw banana bread at my dad, I recognized the stress in my life around my caregiving duties for him. I knew I had to do something healthy as a response to the banana bread incident. I let go of my old habit of trying to do everything by myself and I sought help. I reached out to family and a counselor, and I started by telling them I couldn't do it anymore. "It's killing me. I'm going to die young like Mom did if I continue on this way."

I began by letting go of managing Dad's finances. Then, I said I couldn't make medical decisions for him anymore. I let that go. Then, I said I couldn't be responsible for his estate after he died. (Yes, that was assigned to me, too.) I let that go. I couldn't be Dad's caregiver anymore.

Letting go *was not easy*. I had been taking care of him for so long. I had taken up where Mom left off when she died twelve years earlier. I was standing in Mom's shoes, but those shoes didn't fit me emotionally anymore. They were weighing me down. I had to let Mom's shoes go.

I literally had an old pair of Mom's shoes in my closet. Seriously. At that point, they were twelve years old. (The San

Antonio Shoe Company makes shoes that last a long time!) I had worn them off and on in the summers. A pair of red sandals with turquoise leather weaving. On their soft leather soles, you could see imprints of my feet, the same place where my mom's feet had been.

I gathered up the legal paperwork that had been sitting on my desk for those twelve years. On the phone with my sister-in-law, I said, "I can't have these papers sitting on my desk anymore. I can't have them in my house."

"Put them in the mail to me," she encouraged.

Breath stopped in my throat, "Okay, but you don't have to take up this stuff either. None of us do. We can figure out how to go about this whole thing in a different way so that none of us feel responsible for everything."

I took the papers, stuck them in a big yellow envelope, and couldn't run fast enough to the mailbox.

After I mailed them, I wished I had burned them instead. I also had a moment of panic when I feared Dad would die.

Later, I went to my closet, took my mom's red pair of SAS sandals, walked outside, and threw them in the trashcan. "Goodbye, Mom. That was your choice, and it's no longer mine."

I looked at the sandals, sitting side by side on top of the bags of trash. I snapped a picture with my phone. Was this happening? Yes. This was happening—I was throwing away Mom's shoes. My hands shook as I closed the lid to the trash.

Letting go of taking care of Dad put me in free fall for a while. I didn't really know who I was because taking care of him had been such a big part of my life.

I liken my experience to a story by a rabbi named Edwin Friedman.[1]

One day, a man was going somewhere, walking across a bridge. Another man ran up to him and said, "Can you hold my rope?"

The walking man said, "Sure" and took one end of the rope.

The other man took the other end of the rope, tied it around his waist, and jumped off the bridge.

The walking man was no longer walking. He was standing there holding the rope while the other man dangled on the side of the bridge, over the waters of the river. He called down, "Sir, will you please climb back up? I have places to go."

The other man didn't respond. He just hung there by the rope around his waist.

The walking man called down again. "Sir, I'm going to pull you up." He tried, but the man was too heavy. It wasn't possible to pull him up. He called down a third time. "Sir, do you have a knife? Perhaps you could cut yourself free."

The other man didn't respond.

The walking man (still no longer walking), stood there for three days. He held tightly to the rope, feeling trapped.

Finally on the third day, he knew he had to let go. He had places to go. He was hungry and thirsty. He was tired. He was worried about the other man, but he couldn't stand there for the rest of his life, so he let go of the rope. He watched as the other man fell into the river, and then, the walking man continued on his way.

A few days later, the man with the rope appeared on the bridge again. He was soaking wet after going for a swim in the river and he was searching, asking other passersby to hold his rope.

This story perfectly describes my dad's and my relationship. In some ways, I felt like the man holding the rope, caregiving for my dad. I worried about what would happen if I let go of the rope. I even thought Dad might die if I were to let go, but he didn't. He found other people to carry his rope and care for him. You'd be surprised what a person like my dad can get random strangers to do for him. After I stopped being his caregiver, he had people coming over to make him breakfast!

In other ways, I felt like the man dangling off the bridge. I understood myself as Dad's caregiver. It was part of my identity. I had to cut myself free from that identity (and go for a swim) to live the rest of my life. I needed to learn who I was and how to take care of myself.

Here's your sticky note for this chapter:

What roles do I play in my family?

Do I have to play those roles?

If not, can I cut myself free?

Chapter 10

Stress is a Feeling

This topic deserves its own short chapter because many of us lose it when we feel stressed out. There's lots of information about the stress response in the body (such as heightened heart rate and alertness). But there are also sadness responses in the body (usually a lump in the throat) and happiness responses in the body (usually warmth and a tingling sensation). We have a biological response to all feelings, including stress.

So I'm adding stress to our list of feelings. And to review, here's what we can do about it. First, we feel what our body is feeling, and we put words to it, like this:

"I'm feeling muscle tightness in my chest, like I can't breathe."

"My shoulders and neck feel tense."

"My jaw is clenched."

"My head is hot."

"My stomach is upset."

These are all common bodily reactions people experience when they are about to lose their tempers or when they feel stress.

After you notice these sensations in your body, name the feelings. Pick a few feelings words because they make you stop and think for a moment, which is a good thing. Like this: "I'm feeling stressed, sad, and angry."

Remember, don't say, "I'm sad" or "I'm happy," or "I'm stressed." Instead, say, "I'm *feeling* stressed." The feeling is not you—not your whole being—it's just something you are feeling.

After you name your feelings, tell yourself that you're safe. "I'm safe." This is important because the feeling of stress is usually accompanied by the feeling of being unsafe. So remind yourself that you are safe, that this is a feeling you can handle.

Finally, you can add another reminder that you're loved because when you feel stress, it's common to forget how loved you are. So you can say this whole phrase out loud or in your head, "I'm feeling stressed. I'm safe, I'm loved, and I can handle this feeling."

Do you remember one simple way you can begin to handle that stress response in your body? Try the Perfect Yawn.

Here's your sticky note:

I'm feeling stressed.

I'm safe. I'm loved.

And I can handle it. (Yawn.)

Chapter 11

Doing It Differently Than Mom & Dad

What I'm about to say may sound intense. You might think to yourself, "No way. The person who yelled at me when I was a kid was a jerk!" But one of the milestones in my healing journey was realizing that considering their circumstances, Mom and Dad did the best they could. It was healing for me to think that and feel that deep down in my soul. I absolutely know they did their best.

I've come to see it about myself, too. I was doing my best back when I was screaming at my kids, back when I dumped bubbles on Eva's head, and back when I threw the banana bread. I was doing the absolute best that I could at the time. It doesn't mean that what I did was good, or even acceptable. It just means that with all my experiences and under the circumstances at the time, I did my best.

Thinking this way about my parents and myself came slowly. Eventually, I learned to think of all people this way— that we are all doing the best we can. I learned it first by thinking about my dad.

As a young adult, I did what many young adults do — blamed my parents for, well, pretty much everything. Certainly, for all the bad parts of my life.

One day in seminary, one of our teachers asked us to think about the first time we knew "the world wasn't what we thought." My mind went to a memory about my dad. I was five years old. We had moved to Albuquerque from Dallas, and my poor little brother was getting bloody noses all the time from the dry desert air. And I, being his mostly unsupervised big sister, found it amusing to bop him in the nose on regular occasion to watch it bleed. It made me giggle, how quickly it would start to bleed and how my brother would freak out. It was one of our brother-sister routines.

One day, I walked through the squeaky screen door on the back porch. It was a swinging door, and my little brother, as little brothers often do, trailed closely behind me. The door swung closed, and he walked into it, face first. Not surprisingly, his nose bled. He cried, and my dad yelled at me.

"Jenny! You gave your brother a bloody nose AGAIN!"

"But Dad! I didn't . . . I—"

"This is ridiculous! We can't have this."

I chased down the dark hallway after Dad as he went to get his work boots. My breathing became shallow and a knot formed in my stomach. I looked up at him pleading, "Dad, I didn't do it. Timmy was following me—"

"Jenny, you're going to get a spanking."

74

"Dad, I didn't . . . He walked into the door—"

Dad didn't hear me. He was seeing red, and his ears rang with rage. He took one of his work boots and pulled me by the arm out to the front porch. He sat down on the porch, pulled down my pants, laid me across his knees as he had many times before, and spanked me with the boot. He counted, "One, two, three, four, five, six, seven, eight, nine, ten." With each hit, I whimpered and grunted as Dad's knees pressed into my stomach, stopping my breath. Tears ran down my nose.

Afterward, I pulled up my pants, wiped my nose with the back of my hand, and Dad went to put his work boot away. My heart sank deep into my chest. I was spanked for something I didn't do. I tried to tell the truth, but it didn't matter.

Fast-forward thirty-five years, and there I was, yelling at and spanking my own kids for all kinds of things, even spilt bubbles. Let me say that again. There I was, yelling at and spanking my own kids. I blamed my kids, and I blamed my dad for doing it. Blame isn't helpful because it keeps us stuck in the same old patterns. Once I let go of blame, I began to take responsibility for the things I could, and I learned to forgive my dad because he and I were a lot more alike than I cared to admit. To move on, I needed to forgive him, and I needed to forgive myself, too.

Forgiveness doesn't mean we think the behavior is okay. Forgiveness means seeing the whole person, with all their life experiences, and understanding that they've done their best, and it's no use being mad at them about that. Being mad is just holding you back. Being mad about it makes you focus on blame and how things "should" have been, instead of focusing on solutions in the present.

Dr. Becky Bailey said, "Fear looks to blame because things are not going as they 'should.' Love looks for solutions as it accepts what is."[1] Forgiveness is about love, and this healing journey requires a lot of love and forgiveness.

I learned to forgive my dad by learning more about him and his life. He had it rough. My grandparents raised him and his six siblings. In that house, it was my grandpa who lost his temper as my grandma stood by. Grandpa had it bad; he drank too much, and it was made worse by PTSD from World War II. The family doesn't talk much about the abuse, but I do know my dad was whipped with a belt. "Jenny, one day your grandpa called all six of us over to watch as he whipped your dad with a belt while your dad stood on a chair," my aunt once secretly confessed. Dad never talked about it.

My dad did the best he could, even as he spanked me with his work boot. When he spanked me with his work boot, from what I remember, it wasn't that hard, and it didn't leave a mark. I'm sure Grandpa's belt did. My dad did better than his dad, and I love him for it. I don't love the times he lost his temper, but I accept what happened, and I love and forgive him as a person.

Then I had to learn to forgive myself, to tell myself, "I did the best I could." I had to get help to end those nights of lying awake, thinking to myself about all the times I had failed, and all the things I wished I could change.

Even though all of that was hard, those sleepless nights were a gift. It was the beginning of my healing, because I wasn't comfortable with how things were. Those nights lying awake motivated me to change. There's some shame that's good to simply let go of, but the kind of shame I had was a motivator. It motivated me to move, to do something different, to get help. It motivated me to change my life.

Shame, like all feelings, has power. And that power can be used for good. I let the shame turn to guilt, and guilt is the first step in taking responsibility.

So I decided to do it differently than my parents and their parents before them (and their parents before them). At first, it was uncomfortable. I had some talks with Dad about how he used to lose his temper. I told him I was trying not to do that with my kids. Dad was funny as an old man, and he said he didn't remember losing his temper, but he apologized anyway and said, "Jenny, just tell yourself, 'Children are not for hurting.'" Part of me thinks he forced himself to forget all the hard things in his life because they were just too painful for him to remember.

I also talked to my mother-in-law, the twins' grandma. She spent a lot of time with the kids (and still does), and I tried to show her what I was learning so we could use these strategies together. She felt confused at first, her head spinning with all the changes in the house. In the beginning, when the children misbehaved and I kept my cool instead of yelling, she gave me disapproving stares. She thought we were on the road to raising disrespectful kids. But over time, she saw how as adults, we set an example for respecting each other, and now she's exceedingly gentle with the children.

Finally, I've had many talks with my husband and hundreds of little talks with my kids about feeling our feelings in healthy ways.

And I broke the cycle.

And I pray that one day, if my kids choose to have children of their own, they'll have an emotionally intelligent household, where adults only yell if there's someone in danger, and kids only yell because they haven't learned how to handle their big feelings . . . yet.

And I pray that my kids stay on their big, mature train ride of self-control as they raise their children and make their houses safe and loving spaces. And then the same for their children's children, too. For generations.

The desire to break the cycle is another catalyst for change. I did it and you can, too. Here's your sticky note:

They did the best they could.

I did the best I could.

And now, I'll do better.

Chapter 12

Going Nuts Over the Dirty Can

When you break the cycle, you break free from one kind of "should." It's the kind of should that sounds like this, "My mom and dad shouldn't have raised me like that." Well, maybe that's true to a certain extent—that they shouldn't have raised you that way—but when you use the word "should," you're wishing it were different. You spend time thinking about what might have been.

When you let go of "should," you understand that things happened the way they happened. And you get to choose what you're going to do *now*, in the present. When you use the word "should," you're also holding on to resentment, and when you let it go, you recognize they were doing the best they could.

This can be difficult if you've been deeply hurt. Perhaps holding onto resentment has been a blessing in some ways for you. Perhaps it's been a shield, it's protected you, taught you, and made you strong. Maybe, the resentment isn't helping anymore, and you're ready to let it go. Maybe.

As you consider letting it go, here's a secret about resentment: When you hold resentment for someone else, there's a part of it that's reflected back inside yourself. It's a curious thing, and it feels like magic. Here's what I mean: When you let go of resentment for someone else, it frees up a part of yourself. It paves the way for forgiving yourself. It helps you let go of the "shoulds" you have in your own life. For example, when I let go of the "shoulds" and resentment toward my parents about my childhood, I slept easier and stopped beating myself up over my own personal mistakes. In other words, when I stopped "shoulding" my parents, it made it easier to stop "shoulding" myself.

Even if you don't believe it yet, experiment with the idea and tell yourself, "They did the best they could." Sit with it. Write it down. Talk with a close friend. See if you can find a kernel of truth somewhere in there. See where it takes you.

There's another kind of "should" that used to run rampant in my house. I used to "should" my dear husband constantly. My poor "honey." You know the "Honey Do" list? You can buy them on Amazon. It's a magnetic pad you stick on the fridge. Whenever you think of something you believe your husband should do, you write it on that pad. I didn't have one of those pads on the fridge, but I had one in my head.

I used to think my husband should do many things a certain way—for example, the dishes. Oh, the dishes.

One time, a can of beef grease sat by the sink in my kitchen. You know, when you cook hamburger for dinner and grab an empty aluminum can to drain the grease into so you can throw it away.

Jeff did the dishes that night, and he left the can sitting by the sink. I thought he *should* have taken care of it and thrown it away. "When you do the dishes and there's an aluminum can of beef grease sitting by the sink," I thought, "you should throw that can away." The next day, it was the same story. Jeff did the dishes and left the same can sitting there.

Oh, mama, you know we make ourselves crazy sometimes. That aluminum can. That can!

So I did what any mama would do—the kind of mama with a very big "should" list in her head—I cleaned the kitchen until it was spick and span. And I left the can. There's no way he could miss it now!

But he did! (I can laugh about it now.)

The next day, I threw the can in the trash. Then I turned around and retrieved it. I put it back by the sink. For real. I called my sister. I needed help.

"So there's this can by the sink. Jeff put beef grease in it a few days ago, and I think he should have thrown it away while doing the dishes, but it's like he doesn't see it. I even cleaned the whole kitchen, leaving the can, and he still didn't see it. Or maybe he just doesn't care. I just want him to throw it away."

"Jen, throw the can away. You can do it. It obviously doesn't bother him, but it's bothering you," said my sister.

I thought it should bother Jeff. I thought if I was bothered, he should be bothered, too.

"Jen, throw the can away," my sister repeated.

I threw the can away for good this time. I shut the lid on the garbage container and took a deep breath. Thank God.

This story about the can is just one of many stories. The "shoulds" can (and do) make us crazy.

One day, I coached a group about the "shoulds." A woman in the group wrinkled her brow and said, "My boyfriend 'shoulds' me about everything. He told me I should learn how to kayak, so I'm doing that, but now he's 'shoulding' me about learning karate. I don't want to learn karate. It's making me crazy. How do I get him to stop 'shoulding' me?"

I replied, "This may seem strange, but here's how you free yourself from the 'shoulds' and work with your boyfriend instead of against him. Do you 'should' him?"

"No, I don't. I don't think so."

"Okay. Is there anyone in your life you 'should'?"

She thought for a minute. "No, not really. I don't 'should' anyone in my family."

I looked at her. "Are you sure? Who do you 'should'? How about people you don't know, like a celebrity or someone on the news?"

She gasped, "I 'should' someone from the news all day long in my head."

"Take a news break," I told her. "And try to stop 'shoulding' them. Tell yourself, 'They do what they do.' If you can let go of those 'shoulds,' then you'll figure out what to do about your boyfriend, and there's even a chance that he'll stop 'shoulding' you."

The "should" are like invisible mental viruses. You "should" your neighbor, your husband, the person in the news, and soon after, the "should" come back to you. You end up "shoulding" yourself while dealing with "shoulds" from others.

We make ourselves crazy don't we? "Shoulding" people we *don't even know*. There are several kinds of "shoulds," which I've identified:

1. Things I think I should do differently:
    I should work out more and eat healthier.
    I should be a better mom and have a cleaner house.
    I should take care of my aging parents.

In the past, I should have done (that thing) differently.

In the future, I should definitely do that thing.

2. Things I think others should be doing differently:

   My husband should take out that grease can.

   My kids should respect me more.

   My husband should be a better dad and a better husband.

   My neighbor shouldn't do that thing they do.

   My parents shouldn't have done what they did in the past.

   In the future, my parents should definitely do (that thing).

   That guy on the news should be doing something different, too.

3. Things I think others think I should be doing differently:

   My workout teacher thinks I should go to class more often.

   They also think I should try harder.

   My friend thinks I should try the new diet she likes.

   My parents think I should be doing more for them.

   My kids think I should buy them that trendy thing.

   God thinks I should be a better person and go to church more.

"Should" is what I call a "high pressure" word. Having all these "shoulds" in my head was giving me a high-pressure life! When I learned to let go, I learned to appreciate my husband just the way he is, and a whole world opened up to me.

I learned a kind of acceptance—a peace about how things are. I make choices (and I've made choices in the past), and things are the way they are. For me, I choose to do what's best for me now, and it's best for me to not "should" anyone! Instead, I love. I love on myself. I love on my husband, and I love on my kids. I love on my kids' teachers, our neighbors, and the people on the news. Because I know that everyone's doing their best, and the best difference I can make is if I take care of myself and my husband and my kids, and I trust that love is working.

Love is working to make the world a better place. When we stop "shoulding" and start loving, it creates space to hear others, understand them, and move forward together, like my dad and me. There's enough space for all of us, and there's enough love to go around.

When I stopped "shoulding" my husband, I watched him flourish. He discovered new hobbies and even got a promotion at work. He became a better dad and a better husband. Or maybe he was just that way all along, and letting go of my "shoulds" for him made me stop focusing on who he wasn't, and instead, revealed the love in my heart and the ability to see the best in him, appreciating him just the way he is.

So what do you think? Would you like to break free from all the pressure of the "shoulds"? Here's your sticky note:

Who do I "should?"

For a few days, make a list of all the "shoulds" in your head. For the "shoulds" about others, consider letting them go. For the "shoulds" about yourself, consider each one. Some of those "shoulds" are just ways you're beating yourself up, and there's nothing you can change about those. Let those hurtful "shoulds" go. But a few of the "shoulds" you have for yourself might actually be good ideas. For those healthy "shoulds," are you hurting yourself by *not* doing them? If you've been hurtful to yourself or unhealthy, go ahead and feel guilty for a moment. That "should" has been calling out to you. Let that guilt move you to change the "I should" to "I will." Let a few healthy "shoulds" come into focus, and do what you know you need to do for yourself to lead a healthier, happier life. ("I should stop yelling at my kids" is a good example of a healthy "should" because you're doing it for yourself. Change it to, "I will stop yelling and will learn a new way to raise my kids.")

Chapter 13

The Husband

Women often ask me about my husband, Jeff. They want to know his reaction to this whole thing, this business I'm running helping moms who lose their tempers.

I couldn't have done it without him. When I started experimenting with different ways to discipline the kids, he supported me, and sometimes, he tried some of the strategies too. Today, he says he's "in recovery" from threatening the kids, which means sometimes he slips up and goes there (just like I do).

Jeff told me to tell you, "Here's what I've realized: Threats work in the short term, but they're not healthy in the long term."

Did I tell you I married a great man? If you're reading this book, I'm betting you married a great man, too. Talk to him, mama. Do this together. Ask for his support.

Chapter 14

Bad "Choices"

When you let go of the "shoulds," it's kind of a leap of faith—believing humans are good, that they are doing their best (considering their circumstances). When you let go of the "shoulds," you develop this kind of trust for your kids, too.

I went to a networking meeting for business owners one day, and I met another businesswoman. My introduction went something like this: "Hi, I'm a parenting coach. I help moms who lose their temper."

Sometimes, when I say this, it's seems as if I've become a momentary priest in a confessional. As often happens, this particular mama poured out her heart to me. She didn't start by confessing about her temper, though. She started by telling me about how bad and frustrating her child was. She went on and on as I listened. And then she said, "I keep telling him to make better choices."

I paused and looked at her. Then I asked her the question, "Mama, what if he's not making a *choice*?"

She heard what I said. She understood it to her core. Tears flooded out her eyes—the kind of tears that don't stop. It was like a faucet had been turned on. In that moment, she experienced compassion for her son. She also felt guilt for her reactions to his behavior.

She kept talking through the tears, "I've been so mean to him. I'm always threatening him, yelling, taking his toys away from him—"

I put my hand on her shoulder lovingly, "If he's not making a choice, if your son's doing the best he can, what would you do differently?"

The guilt washed over her and opened her eyes. She beamed with inspiration and opportunity for change, "I'd help him. He needs my help to be successful." She started making a long list of things she'd do differently.

I took a piece of paper and wrote at the top, "He's not making a choice." I recommended that she make notes about things she could do to help her little boy be successful. She had been fighting him all along. It's like the two of them had a script they were playing out every day. They were stuck in the script. I had the privilege to poke my head in and suggest she use her power as a mama and re-write the script. She did, at least for that day. (Re-writing the script takes time and practice.)

When you make the shift and let go of the "shoulds," you know you're doing the best you can. So are others, including your kids. I'll say that last part again: Your kids are doing the best that they can. The best we can do is set good examples for each other and support each other to do good, even when we see—especially when we see—bad behavior.

Dr. Becky Bailey is the author of an amazing Social Emotional Learning (SEL) curriculum for schools and parents. It's called *Conscious Discipline*. She says that all behavior is communication. We know that for babies, right? When a baby reaches up her arms, she's communicating that she wants to be held. When she cries, she's communicating that she wants to be fed or she needs a diaper changed.

Dr. Bailey says that when a child turns two years old, and they start yelling "No!" that it's also communication. The challenge is to avoid taking that word "no" personally. The question becomes, "What are they wanting to communicate?"

If you take a look at your kid and the whole situation (the big picture), what are they telling you? They might be telling you they're hungry or tired. Maybe they're getting sick, or they're worried about something. They might be telling you they feel unsafe or scared. They might be telling you they want connection—to feel loved. They're also probably telling you that there's something they need to learn.

If they're screaming, "No!" because they want to play outside when it's time for a nap, they are feeling big feelings, and it's our job to teach them how to notice. We want to coach them through how to experience their feelings in healthy ways first and foremost, by setting an example. When we yell back at them, we aren't setting an example. In fact, we're responding to our own anger in a hurtful way, just as they are. Instead, to respond in a helpful way, we keep our calm and teach them about themselves, "Sweetheart, you're feeling mad because you want to play outside. You love playing outside."

Our jobs as parents are to attend to needs, to help kids feel safe and loved, and to teach them what they need to learn to become healthy, helpful, and mature adults. Being a healthy, mature adult means knowing how to handle big emotions, and as you know, that takes time. It took me forty years. Hopefully it won't take my kids that long (because I'm setting a good example for them now). I'm teaching them as I teach myself.

What are you telling your family when you lose your temper with your kids? What are you communicating? Do you have a need? Do you feel unsafe? Do you need to feel loved, to be heard and seen? Is there something you need to learn?

Here's your sticky note:

What are they telling me?

What am I telling them with my behavior?

Chapter 15

How to Apologize

When I was a kid, this is how I was taught apologies go, "I'm sorry. Please forgive me."

The response was supposed to be, "I forgive you."

I was forced to say these words many times by the adults around me. Looking back on it now, that's some pretty fast forgiving going on there. And is anyone really sorry when they say this? Is anyone really forgiving someone when apologies happen this way? I don't think so. Forgiveness can be complicated. It's not always easy to see, let alone accept all the underlying hurt and regret in that one moment.

Sometimes, forgiveness isn't necessary. My kids don't usually need forgiveness from me because I love them completely and rarely do I lose any love for them. Forgiveness is good and necessary when there's love lost. I've created my own apology, one without the complication of forgiveness. I call it a low-pressure apology. If you have two children in a fight, it starts by getting them together once everyone's calm.

Have them talk about their feelings. No one's getting in trouble, and each is responsible in some way for what happened. Once they see how their behaviors affected each other, then there's the opportunity for an apology. Here's a basic example.

Brother hits sister, and she decides to tattle, "Mom! Owen hit me!"

"Oh, sweetheart, do you feel sad about that?" (No one's getting in trouble.)

"Yes."

"Do you want to talk to him about it?"

"Yes."

"Would you like me to go with you?"

"Sure."

Eva talks to her brother, "Owen, I felt sad and mad when you hit me."

Responds Owen, "Well, Eva, I didn't like it when you stomped on my foot."

Responds Eva, "Well, Owen, I didn't like it when you were jumping in my face."

"Well, Eva, I just wanted to play with you," Owen says.

"Okay, Owen. Well, in the future, if you want to play with me, please just ask. I don't like it when you jump in my face," Eva concludes.

Sometimes, I'll add, "Kids, in our house, hitting is not okay. I know that I used to hit you when I spanked you, but it's not okay anymore. Our family has values, and we do our best to live by them now. We value each other, and we value our bodies. Our bodies are made to love and be loved. When we hit each other, we're not living by our values."

"Owen, would you like to apologize for hitting Eva?" If he uses the full low-pressure apology, it goes like this:

"I'm sorry. I care about you. I'll try not to do it again."

The response is, "Thank you. I care about you too."

"Eva, would you like to apologize for stomping on Owen's foot?"

"Yes. Owen, I'm sorry, I care about you. I'll try to not do it again."

"Thank you, Eva. I care about you too," would be Owen's response.

The conversation doesn't always go exactly like this, but you get the idea. No one gets in trouble; we just talk about our feelings and values in an effort to work on ourselves and our relationships.

The most important part of the low-pressure apology is what the person who apologizes says. They say, "I'm sorry. I care about you. I'll try not to do that again." Because this is true, right? If you've done something that you feel sorry about and you care about that person, you'd like to avoid doing that again in the future, if possible. Saying you're sorry is acknowledging yourself, the other person, and the relationship between you.

In the case of learning how to be kinder to my kids (and stop yelling at them), apologies were an important part of the puzzle.

Yelling isn't a part of my toolbox for parenting anymore. But I still find the need to apologize regularly.

I only yell these days if a kid's in danger, like they're in the street, and they need to hear me say, "A car's coming! Get to the sidewalk!" But the occasional hurtful cuss word still escapes my mouth.

The other weekend, I woke up after a long night's sleep still tired and worn down. I didn't feel well, and the kids were fighting downstairs. I pulled myself out of bed and stood at the top of the landing and cussed at them. "What the hell are you doing? I'm sleeping, and I wake up to you two fighting? Dammit. I shouldn't have to put up with this shit. I'm taking two dollars out of your allowance for this week— both of you."

Nice way to start a morning, right? Poor kids. But hey, mama's human. *Not perfect*. You know the reason I teach this stuff, right? It's because *I need to learn it myself*. Every day.

The old me would have said the kids were being jerks, or they needed to be "disciplined," so whatever I said, however I said it, I was justified. I would have (mostly) believed they deserved it or that whatever I did was necessary to get them to do what I wanted them to do, which in this case, was to stop fighting. That was the old way—to prompt kids to obey me out of fear, and I made my kids fearful that morning. My little boy ran upstairs to his room, hid himself under his bed, and cried. My little girl hastily went to her backpack and started doing homework at the kitchen table with pursed lips and eyes that wouldn't look up.

But I am breaking the cycle in my family. I don't want my kids to fear me. I want to set an example for them about how good it feels to *not* live in fear, to instead live life feeling safe and loved. And I want my kids to feel safe and loved with me.

After cussing at them, I asked myself, "What's going on with me?" I noticed that I wasn't feeling well. Sleeping for twelve hours and not feeling rested? My throat was sore, too. I must have a cold. Then I apologized. I went to each of them and knelt by their side. I gently touched them and said, "Sorry kids. I'm not feeling so great. I think I'm sick. But still, it's not okay that I cussed like that. It's not your fault."

The kids climbed into my bed, and we snuggled. I call that "double baby snuggle time." It's a special joy you get with twins from the moment they're born. One baby on each side.

"Mom, you teach other moms how not to be mean, but you're mean to us," said Eva.

I responded, "I know. I teach it because I need to learn. I'm not perfect. But you know I've gotten better, and I'm still working on getting better."

Then I told them what I would have done differently if I could have had a "redo." For me, the redo is part two of an apology. That's the part where you talk about or think about what you would have done differently if you could go back and do it again. It's like practice for next time.

"If I had a redo, I would have just woken up and come downstairs to hang out with you while you played. I would have asked what was going on and tried to help solve the problem."

I also asked them if they had a redo, what they would have done to get along better. Occasionally, when it makes sense to do so, we'll have an actual redo, right after the moment. I'll catch myself responding in a way that I don't want to respond, so I stop myself and ask for a redo. If my kids are willing, we'll back up in the conversation, and I'll move forward with the way I want to respond, a healthier way.

When I talked to my kids about the redo, I also told them I changed my mind about the punishment. I wasn't going to take $2 out of their allowance. Punishment doesn't work. It's just another way to control kids out of fear, and it's a perfect example of, "Do what I say, not what I do," because we don't want kids to punish and threaten other people. Punishment is not the way to teach kids respect. Respect is the way to teach respect. You'll find lots of examples of this in Part II of the book.

"I'm sorry about threatening to take $2 out of your allowance. I'm not going to do that. It was a mistake to say it. You know I'm trying not to threaten you that way anymore. It was wrong." A tear escaped my little boy's eye and rolled down his cheek. We snuggled closer.

Let me pause and tell you dear reader, I've come a long way to be able to say things like, "I changed my mind," and "I made a mistake," and "I was wrong." In my house growing up, adults didn't apologize. They didn't change their minds. They were infallible authority figures. They were never wrong.

All of this work has made me understand authority (and adults and kids) very differently. Now I see both adults and kids as simply human. We all make mistakes. And people who are good at authority don't bully others. They take them by the hand and walk next to them, two unique and special human beings working together for good. That's the kind of parent I want to be for my kids. I want to set an example by being the best version of myself, while watching with wonder and supporting my kids as they become the best version of themselves.

There are two sticky notes for this chapter:

"I'm sorry. I care about you.

I'll try not to do it again."

"Thank you. I care about you too."

and

Think about the redo.

Chapter 16

Feeling Pushed Back into the Old Habits

While I strived to break the yelling habit, I went through some surreal moments where I could see what my old reaction would have been, but I wouldn't allow myself to go down that path. I would make a different choice.

One day, I took the twins to the creek near our house and my daughter got mad at me—for good reason. I had put an unreasonable demand on her.

Every day we had gone to the creek, the kids went creek walking with their shoes on (so they wouldn't slip on the limestone bottom). When we got home, we dried the shoes in front of a fan. That day, we were going to grandma's house, so I told the kids, "You can't get your shoes wet today because we'll need them for grandma's house."

Side note: Why, oh why do we do this to ourselves, parents? Why do we make up "have-tos" and "can'ts" when they aren't necessary? Did the kids really need to keep their shoes dry at the creek? No. I've learned to stop myself now before I say "must," "have-to," or "can't." I save those for things that really matter.

My daughter loves the water. She'd be a mermaid if she could. If water's around, she has to touch it, walk in it, be in it. Not to mention, if there are fish or tadpoles, she wants

103

to touch those, too. She's a little mermaid and a biologist. So when I told her she couldn't get her shoes wet, her little world caved in. She screamed at me and lifted her little hand to hit me.

That's the moment when I had an out-of-body experience. In a flash, I saw what my old self would do. I would have grabbed her by the arm, yelled, "WE'RE GOING HOME!" and walked away from the creek, pulling her little body behind me.

I saw how I was feeling pushed back into my old behavior, but I didn't want to be that kind of mom anymore. So, these are the words that came out of my mouth, "I'm feeling pushed back into my old habit. I used to lose my temper. I learned how to do that from my dad, but I'm not going to do it anymore. I'm not going to yell at you, sweetheart."

I didn't yell. Instead, I took some deep breaths, changed my mind about the silly wet shoes, and Eva went creek walking and caught tadpoles that day.

Yelling at her was part of our routine. We were both used to it. When I broke the habit of yelling, it wasn't just about me. My whole family came on this journey, so it was helpful for me to tell the story the way I did at the creek that day, "I learned how to do that from my dad, and I'm not going to do that anymore."

When I first began to rewrite the yelling narrative, I called it the "Anger Bug" because the kids were small. I told them I had gotten the bug from my dad, and that he had gotten it from his dad. I didn't want to live with the Anger Bug anymore. Talking about it with my family has been one of the keys to breaking the habit. It was tough, but talking about it was one way we supported each other.

Over time, as I broke the habit, I yelled less and less. Soon, I was yelling only once a day, then once a week, then once a month. Eventually, when I yelled, the kids were able to say, "Mama, that was the Anger Bug, and it scared me." (They had never been able to say that before.)

It felt like they were pulling teeth out of my mouth at first, but my response turned to, "You're right, sweetheart. I'm sorry . . . that was the Anger Bug. I need to go take a break and calm down." Humility surfaced.

Like I said before, when you have the habit of losing your temper, it's kind of like smoking. Breaking the yelling habit is similar to breaking a cigarette smoking habit. We briefly explored this idea earlier, but here are some specifics:

When you smoke, you get a chemical hit of nicotine. When you yell, you get a chemical hit from naturally occurring chemicals, such as adrenaline. Then you feel relief for a while. Even if you feel guilty, you still feel some relief, like you've blown your lid and let out some steam—some of the pressure that was inside you.

Your family members also get "hits" of adrenaline, and they feel the same relief, like they know that now you've blown your lid, it might not happen again for some time. If you haven't blown your lid in a while, the pressure builds up. Not just in you, but in the whole family. So unconsciously, they'll push you and push you until it does happen, so everyone can get relief from the building pressure.

In this way, your family supports your yelling habit. Just like friends and family enable someone to smoke cigarettes.

Finally, a cigarette smoker usually has a routine for smoking—like first thing in the morning, or the last thing before bed. When work is stressful, or when they visit family for the holidays. The same thing goes for losing your temper: There are usually times of day or days of the week (or certain holidays) when you're more likely to lose it.

I used to lose my temper every morning trying to get the kids out the door for school. I also used to lose it every time I felt like the kids were ignoring me. I used to yell if they didn't hear or obey me the first four times I told them to do something, "Sweethearts, time to get your shoes on. Get your shoes on. Get your shoes on. Time to get your shoes on. PUT ON YOUR SHOES!!!!"

I'm telling you all of this so I can teach you about a concept I call "pushback." Pushback is happening when you get the urge to fall back into your old yelling habit. It happens with cigarette smokers, and it happens with yellers, too. It happened by the creek that day with my daughter. Pushback can happen in different ways. You might feel pushback in your own body, like you need a release, to let off some steam. You might feel pushback from your family members. You might even feel strangely pushed back by a seemingly unrelated event, like a big news story or a family member getting sick.

In coaching, I've seen pushback take many forms. Here's a list so you can start recognizing it:

- *It feels like people pushing your buttons.*
- *Things get on your nerves.*
- *The urge to yell or hurt someone.*
- *Anger or confusion from others (this happens because you're making a change and not yelling and it's confusing to them).*
- *Others get sick.*
- *Others regress (act younger than they are).*
- *You're tempted to regress or lose your temper.*

- *Fear that you will get in trouble.*
- *Doubt (when it comes up, take a few small steps forward to find your courage again).*
- *You have a bigger blow-up than usual (but this time it feels shocking!)*
- *You get stressed out and your body needs more rest (because you're learning and changing).*
- *You get the urge to take on a huge project, or move, or buy a puppy.*
- *Others lose their temper (even people who have never lost it before). When that happens, remind them that was your habit, and it's not okay, not from anyone (it's hurtful and scary).*

Here's the good news about pushback: This is all normal. Pushback can make you want to give up. It can feel frustrating. But here's the secret to moving forward—to breaking the habit for good. When you notice pushback, *celebrate*! Dance. Turn that frustration to celebration.

Talk to the pushback. "I'm feeling pushed back into my old behavior, but I'm not going to do that anymore." Give yourself a pat on the back. Put a gold star sticker on your shirt. Breathe. Say, "Thank you, pushback!"

Because here's more good news: When you feel pushback, that means you're doing amazingly well. You're doing what you've hoped for. That moment at the creek, when I could see what my old self would have done, was an incredible moment. Pushback means you're breaking the habit.

Celebrating pushback is one of the keys to breaking it for good. Here's your sticky note:

Celebrate the pushback.

Chapter 17

Don't Buy a Puppy

If you've read this far, give yourself a giant hug. Really, mama. Put the book down for a moment and hug yourself, or if you're in a public space, close your eyes, take a deep breath, and smile to yourself. You're doing it. I'm so proud of you and happy for you.

When you make the decision to stop losing your temper, you're making the decision to shift the boundaries in your life. Yelling isn't helpful anymore. It's hurtful, and you're going to try to stop doing it. You're not going to put up with it from anyone else, either.

When I told my kids I had the "Anger Bug," and I wanted to try to squish it, that was a big change for my family because I had been the disciplinarian. Yelling was a form of discipline in my house—a way to tell the kids what they needed to do to obey the rules and make me happy. The way I see discipline now has completely changed (more on that later).

As my family made the shift, it was messy. For a while, my dear husband started yelling at the kids. "Well, you're not yelling at them anymore. Someone needs to discipline the kids," he had said.

But my boundaries had shifted, "Honey, no one's going to yell at them anymore. Yelling isn't okay. It's scary. I'm learning a new way to discipline them. Just because I stopped yelling does not mean it's okay for you to start."

We had to learn a whole new way to be parents, a whole to new way to be a family. Confusion, anger, sadness, fear—it all came out. Old stories about me as a kid, old stories about my husband as a kid, about the grandparents as kids (they had alcoholics in their family, too) . . . all those old stories came up. More recent stories about me losing my temper with my kids and my husband came up. "Mama, remember the time when you yelled at us to clean up the Legos?"

"Yes, sweetheart, I do remember. I'm sorry about that."

The stories and the feelings that surfaced were part of the healing process. It helped us to let them out and let them go, so we could grow.

Slowly, we started to take things less personally. Like when I stood at the landing and cussed at the kids the morning I had a sore throat. It had nothing to do with them. Something was going on with me.

And when my dad spanked me as a kid with his work boot, it had nothing to do with me. Something was going on with him.

And when my husband or my kids yell, it has nothing to do with me. Something's going on with them.

More grief and more stories came up, and all of this was unfamiliar ground.

I had one client describe this time as "the earthquake." During a change like this, we all go through something like an emotional earthquake. When I stopped yelling, it felt like shifting ground under my feet. I had never "walked" here before. I had never known family this way. I had never known children and adults this way. I didn't know what to say or what to do.

As I practiced my new skills, I felt like a toddler learning how to speak. I went slowly—slow in speech and slow in making decisions. I changed my mind often, realizing I might go backward before going forward. Sometimes, I would just sit with myself and hold on, or sit with a friend and hold on, or sit with my counselor and hold on, talking about these big changes.

Sometimes I felt scared. I thought I would get in trouble for whatever reason. I worried I would raise disrespectful kids, or kids who needed a lot of counseling. I feared all the "what-ifs," the uncertainties on the road ahead; but I also gained new perspectives on the road behind.

One of my best friends says at times like this, "You're feeling your feelings."

I was an adult woman who hadn't learned to feel her feelings growing up, so those feelings of sadness and worry did feel like an earthquake. They felt big and unmanageable at first.

But slowly, the ground felt more solid as we moved through the process. I learned to walk like a toddler, taking one messy step at a time and falling flat on my face, yelling and threatening the kids at random sometimes.

Then I started to experience some fruits in this new life, on this new earth I was walking on. Letting go of my old yelling habit involved letting go of a lot of old stress too—and surprisingly, I became creative. All of that old stress had been taking up a lot of space in my mind. Freeing up that space made room for a lot more cool stuff. It made room for these ideas and this book!

I became more compassionate toward my parents, my kids, my husband, my neighbors, my kids' teachers, and the people on the news. For everyone.

I noticed stressors in my life and I learned to ask for help. I also learned how to receive the help I had asked for (although that's still one I'm working on).

Another big fruit of this new life was that apologies came easier. I had less worry and more patience.

Most importantly, my relationships became deeper. I learned how to open up more (talking about your feelings will do that).

And best of all, I started to lose my temper less often. Woo hoo!

I see this "earthquake" time as kind of a sacred time for the moms I work with. If you're there, here's what I want to say: "It's okay! You're doing it! This is normal! I've been there, too! Just hold on!" The ground will stop shaking soon, and things will get better and better and better than ever before.

And here's the coaching part: Don't buy a puppy. Meaning, this is not the time to make any big decisions. When you encounter a big shift like this, it's tempting to distract yourself. I've seen women get puppies, move to a different state, quit their jobs, start new jobs, remodel their houses, and take up caregiving for a parent (to name a few). An earthquake isn't the best time to make big changes. So, no new projects.

Don't buy a puppy. This is the time to focus on *you*. Wait till the ground stops shaking. Wait for six months. Maybe wait for a year. Then, if you still want that puppy, that new job, or a remodeled home, then get or do it. Just make sure it's not distracting you from your best life. Make sure you're getting what you want—staying on the road to being a more patient parent, and being the mom you want to be. This is dedicated time to remodel your life and your family. So here's your sticky note:

Hold on! You can do it! No new projects.

Chapter 18

Focus On What You Want

When I coach moms who lose their tempers, they tell me they want to stop yelling, or they tell me they don't want to "blow up" at their kids anymore. They tell me what they don't want.

So that's the beginning. It's good to know what you don't want, but after you realize you don't want something, you need to figure out what you *do* want. What you do want is where you place your focus. You don't focus on the yelling.

Here's why: When you focus on trying to stop the yelling, all your focus is on the yelling. Sounds obvious, but it's a profound truth. You end up in a cycle of yelling, then feeling guilty about it. Hit repeat.

People usually tend to focus on what they don't want. They focus on the negative. When you focus on the negative, you'll be negative. Your eyes and ears are open to the negative. It's what you see—what you experience. So let's stop focusing on the negative.

You want positive things in your life, so take that negative and turn it around. Instead of saying, "I want to stop yelling," see how these impact you:

- "I want to feel in control."

- "I want to be more patient."
- "I want to be a calm mom."
- "I want to feel my feelings in healthy, helpful ways."
- "I want to teach my kids how to feel their feelings in healthy, helpful ways."
- "I want my kids to respect me and hear what I say, and I want to say it with love."
- "I want to have a house where everyone feels safe."
- "I want to have more fun in my life."
- "I want to have more joy."
- "I want to have more peace."

Here's the big secret to having those things: You can have them right now, in this very moment! Maybe it'll be for just one moment, but as you practice, that one moment will expand into another and another. Then, you'll have a whole hour or a whole day where your house is the safe and loving place you want it to be.

There's a simple way you can experience some calm right now. It's the yawning (again). Many people are learning about the body's connection to breathing, and deep breathing is scientifically proven to help people calm down.

There's a show on TV for children called "Daniel Tiger." It's a spin-off of "Mister Roger's Neighborhood." Mister Roger's goal was to teach children how to handle their feelings in healthy ways. There's a song in "Daniel Tiger" about feeling mad. In the first release of the song, it encouraged children to "stomp three times" when they felt mad. But after it aired, it was rewritten. Instead of stomping, the song said to take a deep breath, "and count to four." This is a perfect example of focusing on what you want. If you stomp your feet, you're focusing on the mad. But when you take deep breaths, you focus on being calm.

People are learning deep breaths help—that's reflected by the way the song was rewritten. So the Perfect Yawn (from Chapter 6) plays an essential part in your transformation. In a later chapter (Chapter 25), you'll get a link where you can download and print the Perfect Yawn to hang up at home as a reminder.

When I was little, I was taught to cover my mouth when I yawned, that it was rude to expose the inside of my mouth. I learned to yawn by trying to keep my mouth as small as it could be. But it's helpful if you allow yourself to open your mouth wide—like a lion, cat, or dog. When your mouth's open wide, that tells the body to relax.

Also, in the middle of a yawn, sometimes there's a natural pause. Your body makes you wait before a deep inhale. That's because your diaphragm muscle is releasing. If you'd like to encourage the muscle release, you can put your hand right below your ribcage near the diaphragm. Relish the pause in the yawn, and the release that comes with that perfectly-timed deep breath.

Try taking a few good yawns with a wide mouth and see if you notice a pause before your deepest breath. How does your body feel now? How would you describe your feelings? Name those feelings. They might be relief, peace, relaxed, or even happy.

The other day while I was coaching a woman through this exercise, she started laughing. She said, "I have a hard time relaxing."

I said, "Really? Because you relaxed after a few seconds just now by breathing."

She giggled.

I asked her how she felt. She giggled some more. She said, "I don't know how I feel."

I said, "You're happy. This is what happy feels like. It feels good."

She said, "I feel tingles all over my body."

A tingling sensation is common for people when they feel good, when they feel happy.

You want to feel good. You want to feel good today, and even better tomorrow. That's the simplest way to put it (I think). Here's your sticky note to help you focus on what you want:

What can I do to feel good today and better tomorrow?

Let that be your guide to do what you need to do to feel good, and I'm not talking about good in a temporary sense. This is not the kind of good you feel from eating a chocolate bar. This kind of good is a goodness you feel deep down inside. It's the kind of good you feel when your husband puts his loving arm around you. The kind of good you feel when your kids play nicely together. The kind of good you feel after a long talk with your best friend. The kind of good you feel on a nice walk on a beautiful day. It's joy. It's peace. It's having fun. It's being healthy, helpful, and happy. Feeling safe. Feeling loved.

Chapter 19

A New Kind of Discipline

Before I talk about the new discipline, I think it's helpful to describe the old method. It's the way I grew up. It's the way a lot of us grew up. The old kind of discipline was something we did to children to get them to obey through fear. We motivated them externally with rewards, punishments, threats, and consequences.

Feelings weren't important. The adults reacted to their internal feelings, which sometimes made them hurtful and scary toward the kids. But adults never apologized because adults couldn't do anything wrong. They were always right. Adults focused on the negative: "Stop kicking your feet." They focused on past actions: "I'm punishing you for doing that."

Children were expected to be what adults thought they should be. Everyone experienced a lot of fear, shame, and blame. Everyone worried about getting in trouble. Everyone often felt unsafe or unloved. It was stress-FULL.

The old kind of discipline was something we did to children, but the new kind of discipline is something we do for ourselves (as adults), while teaching our children to do the same for themselves.

Let me say that again: Discipline is something we do for ourselves, while teaching our children to do the same for themselves. Instead of teaching them to obey, we teach children to solve problems in a safe, loving environment. Instead of teaching them to fear, we teach them about values and how to make decisions based on those values.

In the new kind of discipline, there aren't traditional rewards, punishments, and consequences. There are natural consequences—good and bad ones—so children become motivated internally to do the things that will get them the results they desire. (I'll give some examples later.)

Instead of adults being reactive, we're self-aware. Self-awareness and self-discipline go hand-in-hand. As self-aware adults, we recognize feelings as important things that communicate something. We learn how to respond to feelings and deal with them in healthy, helpful ways. Stress is also considered a feeling we can handle.

Instead of infallible authority figures, adults are mentors and models for their kids on how to respond in healthy ways to our feelings and how to apologize when we make mistakes. We all work on problem-solving together as a family, and instead of reacting in fear, we allow our values to guide us.

In the new discipline, our focus is on the positive. Instead of harping on the negative, "Stop kicking," it's "Please keep your feet still," which puts the focus on the positive. We think in the present: "How can I respond to this in a healthy, helpful way?" And our focus is on the future: "What could we do differently if we had a redo?" Our focus is on our values, who we are, and who we want to become—both as a family and as individuals.

Children are guided to become the best version of themselves, not the version adults think they should be. They are accepted and nurtured as the little humans they are, with their own set of values; adults are tasked with identifying, modeling, and teaching the family's values.

With this new discipline, both adults and kids feel safe and loved. They accept responsibility for what they can. They know that everyone's doing the best they can, and they have compassion for people when they make a mistake.

I'm going to talk you through two examples.

First is a little story about crafting with my daughter. We're making bead necklaces at the breakfast table. She hands one necklace to me to tie it off. I tie it and cut off a little bit after tying it. She screams, "Now it's too short! I didn't want you to cut it!!"

The old me would have yelled back, "It's just fine! It's not too short! Go to your room. I'm putting these necklaces away." (Or I'd threaten to throw it all in the trash.) She cries and goes to her room. We don't talk about it again.

Here's the new me (true story): I'm surprised when she screams about me cutting the necklace. I pause and notice my surprise. I take a breath and choose to stay calm. I think about what she's communicating to me. (Remember: All behavior is communication.) She's telling me she's worried about her necklace. In that way, she wants me to see her needs, to connect with her, to love her. She's also telling me that she needs to be taught how to communicate with gentleness (because I don't like being yelled at either). She's also telling me that she needs to be taught how to solve problems with grace.

So first, I connect with her, "You're worried about your necklace being too short." I hold the necklace up and she tries it on.

"It fits me, Mommy. It's not too short." She breathes.

I breathe with her. I'm loving my daughter by noticing her feelings.

Then, I teach her how I would like to be treated. This is a natural consequence of her yelling. She needs to understand that it scared me. "When you get worried like that, please breathe and try to stay calm. It scared me when you yelled. So please talk more gently to me next time." I'm loving myself by honoring my own feelings, and I'm teaching her about relationships.

"Sorry, Mommy," she says.

"Thank you. I love you," I respond.

I also teach her about problem solving for the future. Talking about what she could do differently next time is another natural consequence. I ask, "If I had cut the necklace too short, is that something you and I could fix?"

She nods, *yes*.

I say, "If something like this happens again, let's remember we can fix it."

"Ok, Mom. I love you. I love making necklaces with you."

I'm creating a safe space for my daughter and for her necklaces, which she cares about. Even though I don't feel as strongly as she does about her necklace, I see that she has values that are different than mine, and I honor her values.

I want to create a house where she (and we all) feels safe and loved and trusts we can handle our feelings while we value the things we value.

There were no other rewards, punishments, or consequences as a result of her screaming. We went on happily making necklaces at the table.

One of the big shifts in the new kind of discipline is that you talk about feelings a lot more. It feels strange at first. But when you talk about feelings, it helps everyone feel safe and loved, and that's usually when the issues get worked out. I could have spent my time trying to fix the necklace or punishing her by throwing the necklace away. I also could have spent my time punishing her for screaming. But instead, I took my focus away from the necklace and her screaming (the problems), and talked about the feelings underneath. She was feeling worried. Addressing the feeling was helpful, and that's what the new kind of discipline looks like. When you talk about feelings happening underneath the issue, sometimes the issue just works itself out.

Here's another example. One of my teachers at seminary used to tell this story. His kids were arguing at the table. They were arguing because Daddy served them ice cream, and they each thought that the other kid had received more ice cream in his bowl. He paused and thought about the feelings in the room, and he said, "I love you both equally." Then the boys went on to eat their ice cream happily. Their argument was settled.

When that Daddy paused, he looked under the surface issue of the ice cream. He could have spent thirty minutes working on the surface issue—the amount of the ice cream. He could have joined their argument to tell them "No, I gave you each the same amount." He could have yelled. He could have sent them to their rooms without any ice cream. He could have gotten the ice cream back out and scooped and scooped until everyone was happy (but is that even possible?).

In the new kind of discipline, you try to look past the surface issue. It's like lifting up a rug to see what's underneath. To do this, it takes a moment—a pause. During the pause, you think about what feelings are happening and talk about them.

When you do this, it helps people feel safe and loved and then whatever's happening on the surface—like the amount of ice cream in a bowl—becomes a clearer and easier problem to solve. You see, our brains work better when we feel safe and loved.

Here's your sticky note:

What's the surface issue?

What's the feeling underneath?

There's a phrase people use for the way we're learning to talk about our feelings. They call it "emotional intelligence." The definition for emotional intelligence from the *Oxford Dictionary* is, "The capacity to be aware of, control, and express one's emotions, and to handle interpersonal relationships judiciously and empathetically."

That sounds good to me.

Let's call this "Emotionally Intelligent Discipline." In Part II of this book, I'm going to focus on some specific examples of what it looks like to live in an environment where parents use emotionally intelligent discipline. I'll even challenge you to take it one step further, using emotional intelligence to help you identify and live by your family values.

PART II

Emotional Intelligence at Home

Chapter 20

The Shift

Women have asked me for the "scripts," for the words to say when certain situations come up, like what to say when their kid lies or their kid hits another kid. Part II has more stories from me, and it contains the scripts for you. This will be a shift for your family. A big adjustment. Here's how I suggest you begin. This is your first script. Sit your family down and say this:

"In the past, we've had a house with rewards, punishments, consequences, and threats. Sometimes, we feel scared because we're afraid of getting in trouble. But we're going to try something new. We're going to have a house where no one gets in trouble. We won't have punishments and threats anymore. We're going to feel safe. To do that, we're going to learn to feel our feelings in healthy ways. And when we're hurtful, we'll talk about it, and we'll work on repairing our relationships afterward. Then we'll talk about how to be helpful instead of hurtful next time. We're working on having a kind, loving, healthy, helpful house."

If that's too much and too complicated, try this to begin: "I'm a yeller and I'm trying to stop yelling. I'm going to work on taking deep breaths and feeling my feelings in

133

healthy ways instead of yelling. This is going to be a house where we all feel safe and loved, including me. So to start, when I yell, you can say, 'Mom, you're scaring me. Please take a break and breathe.' I want to be a calm mom with more patience. Will you support me?"

As a family (and as a parent), you'll go over these ideas and practice them many times before it all sinks in. I've noticed it takes about three to six months for most families to believe the new discipline feels natural.

Chapter 21

What To Do When Your Kid Misbehaves

I remember my daughter's first tantrum. She was my perfect angel until one day when she was eighteen months old. I had picked out some clothes for her and laid them out on her dresser. The moment she saw the clothes, she screamed and plopped herself down on the floor in protest.

My breath caught in my lungs. My mouth hung open. I was dumbfounded. Shocked. I didn't know what to do. Over time, her tantrums grew worse, and I came to view them as defiance. I fought for my way. I was in a constant power struggle with a toddler. My days were exhausting because you just can't win with a toddler. Truthfully, there is no winning in a power struggle with anyone. There's only anger, sadness, and frustration.

I'm going to tell you what I wish someone had told me. First, what I perceived as misbehavior is a natural part of childhood. It's called immaturity. It's a stage all kids go through, and as adults, our job is to be there for them to set examples and guide them. We teach them about our family values, and we also teach them about themselves.

Second, what I perceived as misbehavior—as defiance as against me—had nothing to do with me. Stuff was going on with her. When kids have tantrums, it's evidence that the emotional part of their brains are turning on.[1] Eva was telling me her feelings. She just didn't know how to express herself gently, yet (and sadly, neither did I). A baby who cries needs food or a diaper change. A toddler who screams also needs things. A teenager who screams also needs things. An adult who screams needs things, too.

So what does a kid need when they're screaming, or when we see that they're doing something wrong? First and most importantly, they need a calm adult. Here's the script, step-by-step.

When your child misbehaves:

1. Create a safe space and set an example for them. You do this by staying calm. So, breathe. Tell yourself, "What they're doing has nothing to do with me." If necessary, you may need to take a few extra steps to create a safe space. For example, remove others from the room. Or if they're trying to hit you, hold up a pillow and tell them, "This is a safe space for you and for me. Hitting is not okay. This is a safe space." (If someone is in serious danger, call the police for help.)

2. Remember that stress can be contagious, but you're the adult, so you don't need to take on their stress. Calm is contagious, too. Imagine you're on a train; it's

a calm, mature, adult train. You're safe. Remind them they're safe, too. It might be helpful to remind them, "You're not in trouble. We don't get in trouble in our house anymore."

3. If your kids are upset, don't look at them in the eye— they might feel like a frightened, cornered creature and eye contact can feel threatening. Let your whole-body language be relaxed and your voice be gentle. Continue to do your yawn breaths. You're like a mama lion yawning around her pack of lions. The rest of the pack follows suit and yawns, too.

4. Notice their body language. What are they telling you about their feelings? Say out loud, "Your legs and neck look stiff." (Notice what their bodies are doing.) "You're feeling stressed and mad." (Pick at least two feelings words.) By doing this, you're teaching them how to feel their bodies and then name their feelings. Giving a name to the feeling helps the feeling to come up and out. Let them feel their feelings. If you have a child who can name their feelings, simply ask them, "How do you feel?" or "How is your heart?"

5. Notice something positive about their personality. Connect with them lovingly. "You like picking out your own clothes. / You like to be organized. / You

like turning your homework in on time. / You like hanging out with your friends. / You like playing at the park."

6. Pause. Limit the number of words you use. A person who is stressed has difficulty hearing a lot of words. You may even need to pause for a night while everyone rests. You might pause to eat if they're hungry. You don't need to change their feelings. All you need to do is see them.

   (Steps 1–6 may be all that's needed.)

7. If helpful and appropriate, make repairs. Clean up a mess, apologize, solve the problem (if there was one). Help them. This is not punishment. Making repairs is a natural consequence. It's a good, happy, healthy thing to do because after you make repairs, you feel better—you feel whole again. This is also an opportunity to share your feelings with them. Tell them you feel sad about what happened without blaming or shaming them. Sharing feelings is a part of repairing your relationship. If you're struggling to make repairs together, go back to steps 1–6. Or take a break. Repairs often happen after everyone has settled down.

8. Teach them your family values. For a list of family values, visit this special hidden link on my website: jeanettehargreaves.com/values and print the page. Circle your values. Talk about them. Use them to guide you.

9. Plan for the future. If you all had a redo, what would you do differently?

10. Celebrate! Talk about how you all calmly worked on the problem together. If your child was able to calm himself or herself down, notice and acknowledge it. "You calmed yourself down." Put on a favorite song. Dance. Pat yourself on the back. It feels weird at first, but celebrating the small wins is important in breaking the yelling habit for good.

Emotional intelligence focuses on what we want. It's affirming and positive. When we're hurtful, we work on making repairs and figure out what we'd do differently in the future. And we believe that everyone's doing the absolute best that we can.

Even though it might not feel like it at first, practicing emotional intelligence at home is strict. It's stricter than the old way of discipline that carries punishments and rewards. In an emotionally intelligent house, kindness is king, and everyone in the house (including the adults) tries his or her best to live by those values.

A child who has experienced a lot of stress might benefit from extra support from a therapist. If that's the case, it's a good idea for at least one parent to see a therapist, too. A list of helpful professionals includes doctors, counselors, massage therapists, and even nutritionists. Keep looking for support until you find someone you trust who can help you, and find someone for your child whom they enjoy working with.

Before I started working on my own yelling, I thought it was just my daughter who had the problem. I took her to a counselor. It didn't help. Eventually I realized that I needed help, too.

When I stopped yelling, my daughter's tantrums grew worse at first. She was so afraid of getting in trouble, and she was used to getting yelled at or spanked. She had a lot of tantrums before she started settling down and realizing I was not going to get upset anymore. She was not going to get in trouble. I used to tell her, "Honey, I'm going to stay calm, and you're not going to get in trouble."

Writing this to you right now, tears are welling up in my eyes. My heart hurts. I'm sorry for those times when I yelled at my little girl and when I spanked her. If you're feeling sad or guilty, it's okay. Let those feelings come up. We've got to feel our feelings to let them go. If you do feel guilty, it's a good thing if you let that guilt motivate you to change your life for the better. I meet moms who feel just fine yelling at and spanking their kids. It works for them. If they don't have guilt, they don't have the desire to change. Let your guilt be your wisdom—a little voice that says, "It's time for a change . . . "

Most of the work to be done sits within yourself when your child misbehaves. When I first started down this path, the words and actions felt strange, but over time, I became a (fairly) emotionally intelligent mom. You become what you practice. Practice these steps one day at a time to get there.

One last note. Before you take any of these steps, ask yourself if your kids really are doing anything wrong at all in the first place. For nine years, I was a youth minister for a large group of teenagers and their families. Teenagers can be compulsive and wacky—a lot like toddlers. Teenage boys are especially like that old cartoon dog named Goofy, often doing nutty things without thinking, while flailing all over the place.

One day, one of my teenage girls from the youth group hopped on one of the boy's skateboards. She flailed and so did he. She broke her arm. The teenage girl's father came in angry after seeing his daughter hurt. "Where's the boy with the skateboard?" he yelled.

"Sir, he didn't do anything wrong. Your daughter hopped on his skateboard without warning. Both of them were clumsy in the moment," I responded.

He wanted someone to blame, but the kids were just being kids—nothing unusual.

So what if your kids are just being kids? Are they doing anything hurtful? If not, can you let them do their kid thing? Then, attend to yourself. Maybe you have a button that's being pushed. If that's the case, manage your button, calm yourself down, and let kids be kids.

You do a lot of breathing when you're an emotionally intelligent parent. *A lot* of breathing.

To recap, here are the summarized steps about what to do when you see your child misbehave:

1. Create a safe space.
2. Pause and choose to stay calm. Yawn.
3. Ask yourself, "Are they really doing something wrong?"
4. Notice their body language and feelings.
5. Notice something positive about them.
6. Pause for rest or food, if needed.
7. Help them make repairs.

8. Teach your family values.

9. Plan for the redo.

10. Celebrate.

At first, these steps will take a long time, and they'll feel awkward. Eventually, they'll become quick and natural for the whole family. As the mama, your primary role is to be a role model for your values and feeling your feelings in healthy, helpful ways. You'll teach them volumes that way, without ever saying a word.

Chapter 22

What To Do When Your Kid Hurts Another Kid

My kids are sneaky. Out of the corner of my eye, I saw my son shove my daughter. She turned around and hit him. I turned to look at them, and they both looked up at me doe-eyed as if nothing had happened.

I'm pretty good at Steps 1–3 now, so I stayed calm. I asked myself, "What are they telling me they need?" I said to them, "I noticed you two hitting each other. Hurting each other is not okay in this house. Our family has values, and we value our bodies, hearts, and minds. So we take care of our bodies and each other's bodies, too."

"I think you're feeling playful, like you want to wrestle. Wrestling is okay, but you need to do it in a way that doesn't hurt each other." I gathered from looking at their attitudes they were feeling the need to touch and play with each other.

The kids giggled, "Yes, Mama, we want to wrestle!"

"Maybe we could ask Owen's Taekwondo teacher to give you both a lesson in how to wrestle without hurting each other." But they know how to wrestle gently. They do it all the time with my husband. So, that was the end of that. They haven't hit each other in a few weeks. But I'm sure it will come up again.

Please recognize: This is after *a lot* of practice. In the beginning, I used to get angry with my kids and punish them when they would hurt each other. So the first step was to learn to stay calm.

Here are all the steps:

1. Stay calm and create a safe space. If one child is being violent, you may need to temporarily remove the other child from the situation.

2. Children may need a reminder. "You're not in trouble. We don't get in trouble at our house anymore."

3. Practice your yawn breaths. Be the mama lion.

4. Notice their body language and feelings. Help them feel their bodies and say, "Your hands are fists and your arms are stiff. / Your face looks warm and your jaw is tight." Help them feel their feelings, "You feel sad and mad because your brother took your toy. / You feel frustrated that you lost the game." (Or you can ask, "How did that make you feel?")

5. Notice something positive about their personality, "You like your toy. / You like to win games."

6. Pause.

7. If they're calm, notice, "You calmed yourself down."

8. To help the kids solve the problem, have them talk about their feelings with each other first. Then guide them as they solve the problem. There's an example of this conversation in Chapter 15.

9. The problem-solving in this case might just be planning for the redo, and figuring out what can they do next time instead. Help them focus on what they want. Instead of, "Don't hit me," it could be, "Please touch me gently," or "Please ask permission before you take something."

10. Help them make repairs with apologies. It's likely they both need to apologize to each other. Remember the low-pressure apology. "I'm sorry. I care about you. I'll try not to do it again." And the response, "Thank you. I care about you, too."

11. Teach your kids about your family values. "It's not okay to hit and hurt each other in this house anymore." Talk about your feelings, how it makes you feel sad when they hurt others. "We're learning how to respect our bodies, and we take care of each other's bodies, too. We're learning how to be gentle with our whole bodies, with our voices, hands and feet. Our bodies are made to love and be loved."

12. Celebrate. Offer hugs or snuggles all around. Congratulate each other on the work you're all doing, the work of creating an environment where everyone feels safe and loved.

The second step was to notice their body language and to help them feel their feelings. Why did one child hit the other? Were they provoked? What's the whole story? How does the child who was hit feel? It's likely that both of them are sad and mad. Talk about what happened without shame and blame. Instead, honor everyone's feelings.

If you're in a family where hitting is a daily practice, not hitting each other and being gentle with your bodies will take practice, too. So talk about your feelings, teach your new values, and take it one day at a time. If you practice this every day, within three to six months, you will notice big changes (and remember: don't buy a puppy during this time).

Chapter 23

Tattle Tales

Tattle tales used to be a way to get someone else in trouble. As a big sister, I found myself in trouble all the time because of whatever (*lies*) my brother and sister told my parents. No, I probably did do the things they said. But geez, tattle tales create an air of anxiousness where everyone is just waiting to see who's going to tattle and who's going to get in trouble. Tattle tales don't have power in an emotionally intelligent house.

In an emotionally intelligent house, we teach our kids how to feel their feelings. We also teach them to talk about how they would like to be treated. We don't focus on the negative in the past. We focus on what we want in the future.

Yesterday, my eight-year-old daughter tattled on her brother. She said that he wouldn't let her play on his boys' team at recess. She wanted me to get angry with my son. "Mom, Owen wouldn't let me play on his team at recess."

Instead of getting angry with my son, I asked her, "How did that make you feel?"

"It made me feel sad and angry." (Remember that we've been practicing this as a family for a couple of years now.)

I asked, "How would you like your brother to treat you in the future? What do you want the next time you play on the playground?"

"I want Owen to let me play on his team," she thought about it some more and said, "Or I can play on the other team, or maybe there doesn't have to be teams at all."

Owen, listening to the conversation said, "Or maybe you can organize a girls' team."

"How would that make you feel, Eva?"

"Good," she replied.

Looking back on this story, if I were to add one more thing, I would have told her, "You like to feel like you belong. You like to feel included." Noticing positive things about our kids and showing them their values is a way to help them tune their own inner guidance system so they can make values-based decisions when we aren't around.

Tattles are about the person who comes to you with the tattle, so talk to them about their feelings. The only time a tattle isn't a tattle is if there's something dangerous going on. Then an adult should be told, because the kids need help.

When you teach your kids emotional intelligence, you'll teach them how to feel their feelings and how to problem solve for the future. They'll be able to speak up for themselves and say what they need. With a new perspective on tattle tales, your whole house will feel safer, too.

When a new neighbor kid comes over, they often start off with a tattle. I let them know that nobody gets in trouble in our house. We talk about our feelings, and if someone is hurtful, we apologize and try to do better next time. This effect remains as the kids get older and instead of "tattles," the kids feel safe to talk about more difficult situations, like driving and parties and boyfriends and girlfriends. You want your kids to feel safe so they'll tell you things.

Here are the steps for a tattle:

1. Stay calm and breathe. They're trying to make you angry with a different kid. Don't get on the angry train. Stay on your calm, adult train.

2. Notice his or her body language and feelings. You can say it out loud, "Your face looks sad, and your shoulders are hunched. You look disappointed." Or you can ask them, "How did that make you feel?"

3. Notice something positive about their personality. If someone grabbed something from them and they didn't like it, you could say, "You like it when people treat you gently and ask for something first." Whatever's bothering them, it may seem small, but it

might be meaningful for the child. Honor their experience and their feelings.

4. Pause and breathe.

5. If appropriate, help them solve their own problem and make repairs. Coach them on what to say so they can teach others how they'd like to be treated. "I felt sad when you grabbed my pencil. Next time, will you please ask me for it first?"

6. If you've been living in a tattle tale-infected house, where the other kid always gets in trouble, that child might be upset and frightened when a tattle happens. Help them feel safe and remind them that no one's getting in trouble anymore. We're just talking about our feelings.

7. Talk about the redo. Instead of tattling, what might they do next time? When is a good time to "tattle" (to ask for help) and when is it not? Teach your values.

8. Celebrate. If you used to let your kid get you worked up over a tattle (and you didn't this time), allow yourself to smile. You're doing it!

Once kids feel their feelings, that might be all they need, or if there's a problem to be solved, it becomes much easier to solve after the feelings come out. Those heavy feelings, such as hurt, disappointment, and anger weigh us down. We get creative with our problem solving when we let those feelings come up and out and let them go.

Chapter 24

When Your Kid Lies

When I was a kid, I lied to my parents when I was scared of getting in trouble. When I was a teenager, I lied to my parents when I was scared of getting in trouble. So if you want your kid to tell you the truth, this is how you do it: You make your house into a place where no one gets "in trouble."

In the last chapter, we talked about tattles and I provided some examples about how to create a house where no one gets in trouble. In my house, we talk about our feelings and our values. We talk about what we might like to do differently next time. Sometimes, if we've been hurtful, we apologize. If there's a mess, we work together to clean it up. No one gets in trouble.

In an emotionally intelligent house, we recognize that everyone messes up sometimes, even adults. There's space for grace. There's space to say, "I'm sorry. I messed up. I want to do better next time."

If an adult lies to another adult, they're not punished. They don't get grounded. They don't get their phone taken away. The adults talk about it (and they may go to counseling). They talk about their feelings, about what led to the lie. One adult might lose some trust for the other adult for a while. That's a natural consequence. They work on their relationship so it can get better. They both work on getting healthier.

And that's what we want for our children, too. When my kids were little, I experimented with all the punishments, from yelling to spanking to time-outs. They got in trouble all the time. They were scared, and my little girl used to lie to me all the time, about tiny little things every day. At first, I got mad at her for lying, and I got mad about whatever she was lying about, too.

When you get mad at a kid who lies, it doesn't make them into a truthful kid. It just makes them want to lie better next time.

So why does a kid lie?

1. They're afraid of getting in trouble.
2. They wish they had made a different choice.
3. They're worried you might not love them if you knew the truth.

If your kid's used to lying (and you're used to getting mad about it), it's going to take time to break this habit, and it starts with you. Here's how I worked with my little girl. When I caught her in a lie, I told her, "You used to get in trouble for lying, but we're not doing that anymore. You're safe with me

now. I love you, no matter what. You can tell me the truth."
Then I asked her how she felt.

"I'm scared, Mama." Sometimes she would tell me with words, or with hunched shoulders and tears in her eyes.

"That makes sense that you feel scared. It's okay, sweetheart. I love you. I'm sorry I used to get mad like that." Then, I breathed. Sometimes I held her and kissed her sweet face.

I did this over and over. I told her, "You're not going to get in trouble for lying anymore." I said this roughly forty times before she stopped lying to me daily. It took that long for her to know she was safe, for her to know that she didn't have to lie any more.

We were breaking our habits. I let go of the habit of getting angry over a lie, and she broke the habit of being scared to tell the truth. During that time, we didn't even talk about whatever she lied about. Instead, I focused on what I wanted—on the kind of relationship I want with my daughter. I want an open, honest, loving relationship for her, and for all of us in the house.

Sometimes, I said, "Sweetheart, I feel sad when you lie to me." She felt her fear, and I felt my sadness. I told her over and over, "Next time, Sweetie, you can tell me the truth and it will be okay."

Lying isn't misbehavior. It's communication. Your kid's telling you something. Like maybe they're scared, sad, worried, or mad at themselves. And they're telling you they don't feel safe enough to tell you the truth.

Let me say that again: Underneath the lie, they're telling you they don't feel safe enough to tell you the truth. If there has been a mistake, solve the problem together. Apologize for hurt feelings. Pay for something that's broken. Create a safe space and teach your child how to reconcile and move on. Help them reconcile with the problem, with you, and with their own feelings.

Growing up, my bedroom had a fancy door decorated with windows and a curtain. When I was ten years old, my brother and I had a fight one morning before school. Mom and Dad weren't around because they had already left for work. My brother chased after me as I raced to my room and tried to slam the door. But before the door shut, my brother raised his fist to hit me. Instead of hitting me, he hit one of the windows on my door. It cracked.

The blood left my face, and I felt like I was going to throw up. Panic set in. I quickly made a paper sign that said "Jenny's Room" and taped it up over the cracked window. I used a whole roll of tape. For months, I lived in fear, worried my parents would find out.

I wished I had made better choices. Every time I went into and out of my room, I saw the sign and the little cracks in the glass behind it. My heart weighed heavy. "Stupid, stupid, stupid. Stupid brother. Stupid for fighting like that. I was so stupid for slamming the door. Stupid door with windows. I hate the windows. I hate my door. I hate my dad. Mom and Dad can never find out!" I made more signs and taped them on the door.

The cracked window haunted me and made me a nervous wreck at home. I often wanted to cry. Sometimes, I anxiously stood in front of it, hiding the cracked glass behind the sign and behind my body, distracting Mom and Dad so they wouldn't see it. "Dad, what are you doing in the hallway here outside my door?"

For a year of my childhood, I couldn't breathe easily in my house. I was afraid, and then one day, my dad noticed it.

"Jenny, your window's broken. How did that happen?"

"I . . . I don't know."

"Well, we'll have to fix it."

I held my breath.

At dinner, he told Mom, "Jenny's window is broken," he turned to me and asked again, "Do you know how it happened, Jen?"

I gagged on my spaghetti and whispered, "No. I don't know."

Dad replaced the window. I followed him around and watched as he took the door off its hinges, laid it on a big table, took out the broken glass, and replaced it with a new piece of glass.

"So you don't know how this happened?"

"Nope. No idea."

If he was mad, he didn't show it, although I'm pretty sure he knew I was lying. I felt I got lucky that time—not getting yelled at, not getting spanked.

I grew up in a house where kids got in trouble all the time. If I broke a plate in the kitchen, someone yelled at me. My parents loved their plates, and they lost it when they were broken. Sometimes, I got in trouble for things I didn't do. So I lied about lots of stuff that happened. I worried all the time about getting in trouble.

If I could go back and change everything, I'd have a dad I felt safe around. I would have said to him, "Dad, I got in a fight with my brother, and a window broke on my door. I'm feeling nervous. I feel bad about it. Can we fix it? Can I help? I'm sorry." Maybe we would have talked about fighting with my brother. Maybe I could have helped him fix the door, or I could have helped pay for the glass.

So when do you start with your kids? Start now. Help your child feel safe telling you the little things. Then as they get older, they'll feel safe telling you the big things, the thing about the ding on the car, the thing about the rough night at a friend's house.

Even if your child's older, it's not too late. Make it so that you and your house are a safe place.

One of the rewards of creating a safe relationship with your child is that as adults, your children will be more likely to choose friends they feel safe around, and they'll have a family they're honest with, too.

As parents, our small actions have ripple effects, and it's never too late. So start today. When your kid lies, hold them, love them, tell them it's okay. Breathe and work on it together.

Here are the steps:

1. Stay calm. Breathe. This is a safe space and no one's getting in trouble.
2. Notice their body language. They're probably sad and scared. Talk about it. "You're feeling scared because

you're worried you'll get in trouble. You're not in trouble, Sweetie. I love you."

3. Notice something positive about their personality. If they were doing something sneaky, notice what they like, "You like to hang out with your friends. / You like to eat candy. / You like little shiny things."

4. Pause. Breathe. Make time for them to feel their feelings.

5. Make repairs. Is there a problem you can work together to solve? Help them clean up a mess lovingly. They might need help with healthy boundary setting. They may need to apologize. You may need to apologize, too. "I'm sorry I've gotten mad about this in the past." Tell them your feelings, about how you've lost some trust for them, or about how you feel sad. Tell them your feelings without giving them shame and blame. They've lost trust for you because of the way you used to get mad. The point is to help you repair your relationship and build respect between the two of you. Assure them you love them, even with this knowledge of whatever they've done. They may be punishing themselves by looking down on themselves. Punishment doesn't help someone to live by values. Love does.

6. Plan for next time. If this situation happens again, what does the redo look like? How can it be happy, helpful, and healthy for all of you?

7. Teach your values. You value openness and honesty. You value working together to solve problems. You know everyone makes mistakes, so we lovingly work together to solve problems.

8. Celebrate. Hugs. Deep breaths. Re-tell the story about what happened when the truth came out, how you worked together. Share the success story with your friend or husband. Write the story down. This is the new path for your family, the way you want to move forward.

Chapter 25

What To Do When Your Kids Won't Listen

Mamas tell me, "But Jeanette, I yell at my kids because they won't listen. I tell them something five times and then I yell. Then they do what I ask them to do."

First, go back and read that sentence again.

Imagine yourself and your kids. They're playing in the living room. You're telling them to clean up their toys from the kitchen because it's time for dinner. You tell them four times. The fifth time, you yell. They clean up.

This is your script. You and your kids have this routine. It's a habit. It's simply the way you are doing it at your house, and it doesn't have to be done this way.

To begin, you're telling yourself, "My kids aren't listening to me." This may not be true. You know how sometimes when you're on your phone doing something, you can't hear anyone else? It's the same with kids. Maria Montessori called a child's attention the "cycle of activity." Children's brains are learning so much. They might be holding a rock in their hand. They might be staring at light reflecting. They might be washing their hands. Their whole attention might be on that small little thing. Their whole body, heart, and mind are focused on learning something while the soap bubbles run down their fingers, and they can't hear you. They don't hear you. They're not ignoring you. They're not being disobedient or defiant. It has nothing to do with you.

We adopted the phrase "cycle of activity" at our house. When someone asks us to do something in the middle of an activity, we say, "I can't right now, I'm in a cycle of activity." For example, if I'm washing the dishes, I'll finish washing the dishes before I make a sandwich for someone who's hungry. I also try to notice when my kids or husband are in a cycle of activity. If they are, I try not to interrupt them.

For a child, a cycle of activity can last a long time. Some children can spend three hours pouring water out of a cup over and over (Maria Montessori said the longer the cycle, the more they're learning and the deeper their learning goes.) When my kids are in a cycle of activity and it's time to do something else, I'm thoughtful about how I interrupt them. To you, whatever they're working on might not seem like a big deal. To them, it might mean everything.

Secondly, even if they do hear you, in your family, the routine is that they obey you only once threatened. That's your routine. So in the new kind of discipline, your child will still be obedient, but now they'll obey because they feel connected to you. Here's how. First, stop yourself before you say any of these classic scripts:

"Do it before I count to three!"

"Do it or else!"

"Do it or you'll get a spanking!"

"Do it. Do it. Do it. DOOO IT!!!!!!"

"Do it and I'll give you a treat!"

Instead, try this out as a new script for your household to get the kids to listen to you. It's about connecting with them first before giving them a direction. I call it "Connect & Direct."

1. Breathe. Stay calm.

2. Go to where your child is. Touch them lightly. Make eye contact. Say their name. Notice what they're doing, "You're working hard on this."

3. Notice something positive about their personality. "You love this activity." Notice their feelings. Steps 2 and 3 are where you connect.

4. Then, it's time for you to "direct." Tell them it's time to change their activity. It might be to get their shoes on, wash their hands, or get ready for dinner. "Now it's time to get ready for dinner."

5. If they're resistant, breathe. Notice their feelings. They might be feeling sad or frustrated about needing to

switch to a different activity. You understand that because you don't like switching activities either when you're in the middle of doing something. Ask them, "How much time do you need?" Try to give them that time. If there's a mess from their activity (but they'll come back to it later), perhaps they can leave the mess for a day until they get back to it. Remember that this might be a big deal for them (even if it seems small to you).

6. If they're still resistant to switching activities, teach them your family values. Your family values being to school on time out of respect for the teacher. Your family values eating dinner together. "In our family, eating dinner together is important because it's one of the ways we spend time together."

7. Go back to staying calm and noticing their feelings. Say positive things about them, about how their work is important to them. Repeat steps 1–3 and try to make a connection.

8. Celebrate. When you connect with your kids and get them to do what you need them to do, smile to yourself. Pat yourself on the back. Dance in the kitchen. Feel good.

At first, it seems like connecting will take too much time, and in the beginning it does take time, more time than the yelling and threats. Like my husband said, "Threats work in the short-term, but they're unhealthy in the long-term." Especially during this time of transition when you're re-writing the scripts in your family, "Connect & Direct" will take more time. You've used yelling and threats to get them to obey you out of fear in the past, so your kids aren't used to obeying you out of a feeling of connection. So go over these steps with them. Read it straight out of this book. Tell them you're not going to yell anymore when it's time to clean up.

Eventually, when you've created your house where everyone feels safe and loved, it won't take so much time. It'll be easier because when a child feels a regular connection to you, they're more likely to do what you ask. You're more likely to happily jump into a task assigned to you by a boss you love at work, and you're likely to grumble and procrastinate over a task assigned to you by a boss you dislike. Your kids are the same way. Once you've created a house where no one gets in trouble and everyone feels heard and respected (including yourself), your kids will be much more likely to happily do what you ask them to do. So how can you tell you've made a connection?

Connecting with someone is like tuning into an old-fashioned radio. You pay close attention and tune the knob until you're hearing them clearly. I made a connection with Eva at the dinner table the other day. She was showing me a picture she drew.

"Look at this, Mama."

"You've had fun coloring this picture. You used a lot of purples and blues. You like those colors."

I had tuned in. Her face lit up. "Yes, I also like the color orange, and I like the trapeze, and I like playing with my friends," she said as her feet swung happily under the table. She made eye contact with me and smiled.

When you connect with someone, they learn about themselves. It's good to have kids who know about themselves because it will help them make choices based on their values and their good character when you aren't around to guide them.

Sometimes when you connect, a person will become emotional. There are days when Eva will come home grumpy from school, and she seems to be angry about everything. I slow down and breathe and ask, "Sweetheart, are you okay? Did something stressful happen at school?" Sometimes she'll just cry. When that happens, I comfort her. We don't solve any problems. I just help her soothe herself.

I made a PDF for you called "Connect & Direct." Use the simple steps to connect *before* you give your child a direction, like cleaning up his or her toys. First connect, then direct. Connect, then direct. Pay close attention to what happens when you connect. Do they light up? Do they talk more about themselves? Do they look pleased? Do they get emotional? How can you tell you've made a connection?

There are some tips about giving direction on this PDF, such as when you give a direction, you'll want to show the child the big picture—how the thing you're asking them to do is connected to your family values. This PDF has two pages. The first page is how to connect and the second page has the steps for the Perfect Yawn (as I promised earlier). Remaining calm is an essential part of connecting, so that's why it's included. Here's the link.

jeanettehargreaves.com/connect

Out of all the scripts, Connect is the primary script. It's the script from which all the other scripts flow. Master this one piece of emotionally intelligent parenting, and the other parts will become instinctive. That's why I made the PDF.

At this point, your house might have a lot of sticky notes and PDFs posted all over. That's okay. It's a good thing. You need all these reminders for now. One day, you won't need them anymore, and your house will look normal again. This is a messy process, changing from one kind of discipline to another, but it's worth it.

Chapter 26

When Someone Else Yells

In our house, I was the yeller. I was considered the disciplinarian. The kids were afraid of me. My husband stayed quiet and looked to me whenever they misbehaved. When one or more parents yell, the kids take their cues from them and they often become yellers too. So our daughter yelled a lot, and our son yelled too.

When I stopped yelling, it confused my husband Jeff. because I didn't have the steps clearly laid out for me (as I've laid them out for you in this book). But I asked for his support, and he gave it. He watched as I experimented and developed this way of values-based emotionally intelligent parenting. It was messy at times, but eventually we agreed that yelling wasn't the way we wanted to parent.

Over time, we also taught the kids that it's not okay for them to yell. As they grew older, we became role models for them, showing them how to handle our big feelings in healthy ways. (What parent doesn't want to be their children's role model?) We helped them figure out the ways they use to help themselves calm down. We practiced calming down together.

Here are some examples of how we calm down in healthy ways in our family. For me, breathing, exercise, sleep, time outside, talking with my counselor, and spending time with friends helps. For my husband, bike riding and listening to music helps. For my daughter, snuggling with her blanket, hanging from the trapeze, and chewing gum helps. For my son, snuggling with his stuffed animals, biking, and playing with his cars helps.

I used to do a lot more unhealthy things like yell, drink too much wine, eat too many processed foods, watch too much TV, spend too much time online, and gossip and complain. Those things appeared to calm me down, but in actuality, I was just numbing myself, withdrawing from my family, myself, and my feelings. The healthy ways of calming down are truly soothing, a way to nurture your soul and make you feel good deep inside.

What soothes you? What nurtures your soul? How about your family members? What soothes them? Knowing this will help you know how to address the yelling.

When someone does yell, here's how I handle it now.

1. I stay calm. I breathe.
2. Underneath the upset and anger, someone who's yelling is usually scared. So I don't look at them in the eye. I use a non-threatening body posture.

3. They're also usually sad. Their feelings have been hurt. So I'm gentle with them.

4. I notice how they're feeling. I notice something positive about them. For example, "You're feeling upset that you weren't included. You like to feel included." I comfort them (sometimes they cry), or I suggest they comfort themselves by doing one of the things that soothes them.

5. If it's appropriate, I help them problem solve.

6. I help them make repairs. I show them I love them and give them a hug.

7. Later, if it seems helpful, I tell them how the yelling made me feel. "It's scary, and it would be nice if we could solve problems next time while staying calm."

8. I also try to figure out if I was putting too much pressure on the person. Did I play a role in their outburst? Sometimes we talk about how we can work better together in the future.

After a stressful moment like that, I breathe. I might take a walk or call my counselor to soothe myself. If I have any feelings of stress, sadness, or anger, I let them come up and out, but I don't shame or blame the person who yelled. My feelings are my responsibility.

Chapter 27

What To Do When Your Kids Annoy You

When I lead workshops, I ask the mamas what annoys them and how it feels. The reason I ask this is because annoyance occurs before you lose your temper. Many report they feel annoyed, then more annoyed, and then super annoyed. That's when they lose it.

When you're in the habit of losing your temper, you're also in the habit of feeling annoyed a lot. It's likely that whatever annoying thing the kids are doing, it's the last straw on top of many other things that were annoying you before they began their behavior. So I'm going to give you lots of ideas on how to handle this. As I've taught you, when a feeling comes up, like you're feeling annoyed, the primary person to work on is you.

The House

Perhaps you're waking up feeling annoyed. What annoys you around the house? Make a list. There could be something going on with your body, like an injured foot or back. There could be an object that annoys you, like a fan that squeaks. Perhaps you don't get a shower every day. It might be an unpaid bill. It might be that you never see your husband who works many hours.

I was having trouble sleeping, and it annoyed me. I thought about it, and I realized that I wanted my door open so I could hear the kids, but the nightlight from the hallway was keeping me awake. My solution was to put up a curtain over the doorway, and I slept much better! I felt less annoyed at night and also during the day because I slept better.

I also realized I was sensitive to noisy battery-operated toys. They annoyed me. So we took batteries out of most of the toys. After that, we tried to buy toys that didn't use batteries.

I also realized I was sensitive to some of the old-fashioned children's stories—I didn't like reading those books to my kids. So I created a library for my kids I felt good about with categories like nature, science, history, and some fiction—but fiction I felt good about. When the kids were young, I read each book before putting it on the shelf and asked myself if it reflected our family values.

Work on tackling the things that annoy you one at a time. If it's something small, it might take a few minutes to remedy. If it's something big (like a large, unpaid bill), it might take longer to figure out. For example, changing over the children's library in my house took several months.

I talked with one mom who never got to see her husband because their work shifts differed. They saw how it drained their relationship, so her husband took a different job. Now they're happier and they breathe easier. What can you do to help you breathe easier so you wake up feeling better each day?

The Husband

Is there something about your husband that annoys you? One of the most common annoyances I hear from moms is that Daddy puts the kids to bed differently. The way my husband used to do things also used to bother me. So to change my mindset, I created a simple phrase: "Daddy Do." As in, "Daddy do what he do." It's a silly phrase and the grammar isn't correct, but it means that Daddy does things his way, and it's okay. It reminds me to stop feeling annoyed about the way he does things differently, and to accept him for the great man he is. This goes back to the chapter about dropping the "shoulds" (Chapter 12). The phrase, "Daddy do" makes me smile, and it helps the annoyance (and the "shoulds") melt away.

In my house, we used to "should" each other all the time, and it was very annoying. After I adopted the phrase, "Daddy do," we all began to use it. If the kids tried to tell me how to do the dishes differently, I told them, "Mommy do." If I tried to tell my daughter how to make her art differently, she told me, "Eva do." When Grandpa came to the house and just wanted to sit on the couch, Grandma and I would say, "It's okay. Grandpa do." They do what they do, and it's all okay. They have their way of doing things, and I have mine.

The Kids

When it comes to being annoyed by the kids themselves, I've realized something. Often, they're mirrors. What I mean by that is they mirror my behavior. So when they annoy me, I ask myself first, "Do I do that?" When the answer is yes, I love on myself and go gentle on the kids. Sometimes, I decide to stop doing that, too (after all, it's annoying!). Just today, I heard my son saying, "Stop it!" to my daughter as she followed him around. "Stop it! STOPPIT!" It was annoying me, and it was exactly the way I used to tell her to stop. Owen was being my little mirror. I simply smiled to myself, shook my head, and let it go.

If the kids aren't acting like you, are they acting like kids? What story are you telling yourself? What thoughts are you having? What if you simply decide to let the negative thought go? Do the full breathing exercise with the Perfect Yawn. Work on feeling good while you let the kids be kids.

Misbehavior . . . or Is It?

Is someone misbehaving? Are they truly misbehaving and being hurtful? If they are, use the steps for misbehavior (Chapter 2). If not, try to get out of your own head and notice how they're feeling. For example, if a kid's being loud and jumping around, maybe they're excited about something. When kids are excited, I've noticed it often annoys adults because many kids show it and their whole bodies say, "I'M EXCITED!!!" When you notice how excited they are, it helps them feel their feelings and calm down.

Being Sensitive

Finally, if you're feeling annoyed a lot, you might be a sensitive person. And if you're sensitive, there's a good chance your kids and maybe your husband are, too. Honor your sensitivity. Here is a list of some things that may help.

Limit your screen time. Try to read positive things instead taking in negative things. Take large breaks (weeks at a time) from the news and social media. Consider the food you eat. What are you sensitive to? Eat healthy foods that give you good energy and make you feel good. Talk to your doctor or a nutritionist about ways to calm yourself physically with food or supplements. See a massage therapist who can help you calm down. Be aware of words—the words you say and the words you think. Words are important because they influence how you feel. Choose words that encourage, love, and inspire you. Think about your schedule. Make time to take care of yourself.

I do all these things. I'm sensitive. As it turns out, my whole family is sensitive. When someone's acting out, I look underneath the behavior to try to figure out what's going on.

Chapter 28

Don't Beat Yourself Up

Mama, you've done the best you could. Consider where you've come from. Consider how far you've come. My kids still tell stories from my yelling days. This journey is part of our story as a family. "Mama, remember that time when Eva dumped bubbles out, and you put bubbles on her head?"

I say my part, "Yes I used to lose my temper a lot. I learned that from my dad, but I got help and I don't do that anymore. I'm sorry about that. I love you." We're all still healing, and we're all still learning how to live and love each other in healthy, helpful ways.

The other day, my little boy said, "Mama, we're coming out of the Age of Consequences."

I asked him, "What's the Age of Consequences?"

He said, "The Age of Consequences was a time when the kids would fight and the grown-ups would get angry."

I said, "Wow, sweetheart. What age are we in now?"

Owen replied, "The Happy Age."

Oh, my little sweetheart. From the mouths of babes!

Being in the Happy Age isn't always happy. But it is an age where everyone gets to feel safe and loved. I still feel sad sometimes about how it used to be, but I don't dwell there. And I don't beat myself up anymore. I did the best I could. I did the best I could, and so did you. And you still are. You're doing the best you can.

Chapter 29

Rewards and Punishments

We've talked a lot about punishments and consequences. In an emotionally intelligent household, there are no punishments, only natural consequences, which is the natural effect from a behavior (good or bad). But we haven't talked about rewards.

Traditional rewards and consequences are intended to control kids, to motivate them to obey through fear. Yes, even rewards are based in fear. It's a fear founded in the idea they won't get the reward if they don't accomplish the behavior. These are external motivations.

In the emotionally intelligent house, kids are motivated internally. Values and good hearts guide them. The family focuses on what we want, how we want to feel today, and how we want to feel in the future. We want to feel good, the really deep kind of good—full of peace and joy. We want to feel safe, loved, healthy, and helpful.

So essentially, there's only one "reward:" It's a natural consequence—that of feeling good. We feel good when we're doing good and being the best version of ourselves. One way we encourage our kids to feel internally rewarded is by noticing the good stuff and celebrating with them.

When my daughter hangs from the trapeze and says, "Look at me, Mama!"

I say, "You look like you're having fun! You're so strong, and you're proud that you can hang that way! You love to swing from the trapeze." She feels good, and that's her reward—a natural consequence. She probably already feels awesome and celebrating with her as her mom just enhances this positive feeling.

When my son shows me a flying side kick from Taekwondo, I tell him, "You love Taekwondo! You're so strong! You feel proud of all the things you've learned." That's a celebration pointing out his values.

When my kid brings good grades home from school, I'll ask them how they feel. They tell me they feel good. Instead of rewarding them, we celebrate as a family. Celebrations are a natural consequence, something that happens organically when good things happen. We show Daddy the good grades and we smile. We tell Grandma and Grandpa. Sometimes we dance.

Celebrations happen no matter what, and they highlight the good. For example, if a grade isn't good, we celebrate other things, perhaps what they learned from that project. We feel good about the good stuff, and we don't let the bad stuff weigh us down (because we're learning from all of it).

Writing these examples, I'm smiling. It makes me feel good when my kids feel good. Feeling good motivates us to do what we need to do to continue feeling good.

For example, the kids are motivated to study their spelling words, because they know a good grade on the spelling test will make them feel good. They're also motivated to tell the truth about something difficult, because they know it will make them feel good afterward. Sometimes, they're motivated to clean up the clutter in their room, because they notice what a nice feeling they have when it's clean. (To motivate them to clear their clutter, I remember that they are little mirrors, and I work on clearing my own clutter first!)

If your kids are used to external rewards, it's going to take practice for them to tune into their feelings and let go of the idea that they will or won't get a prize for doing something good. Here are some things you can do to start.

When they accomplish something and they obviously feel happy, ask them how they feel. If they struggle to find the words, you can describe their body language, "You're smiling and jumping around. You're happy and excited!" Celebrate with them. Point out their values.

There are some schools of thought that say we shouldn't say, "I'm proud of you" or "Good job" to our kids. But we're in relationship with our kids, so it's okay to tell them how you feel. The occasional "Good job" is just fine— just make sure it's how you feel. Because when you say, "Good job," it is about *your* feelings, not about theirs. You're sharing your joy. In addition, make room for their feelings— notice how they feel about their own work. Let their feelings be their primary guide and their own reward.

But hey, everyone likes to hear, "Good job," every once and awhile. If you've read this far in the book, *good job*, Mama! Keep going. You're doing great. Let me celebrate you! Tell me a story about a time when you didn't blow up, like "Today I almost yelled at the kids, but I didn't, instead I—." I want to hear from you. Email me at this address: jeanette@tempercoaching.com. I'll write back to say, "Yay! You're doing it." Not everyone will have made it to this point in the book. You have. Congratulations.

Chapter 30

What's God Got To Do With It?

I presented these ideas to a group of moms. At the end of the presentation, a mom raised her hand and said, "But Jeanette, my kids just won't listen unless I yell." I took a deep breath. I pointed to some of these techniques written on a board at the front of the room. I pointed at ways to connect with the kids so they'll listen. Then I paused and looked around at the women.

I was in a church, speaking with a church group. I took another breath and lovingly said, "Mamas, this all boils down to just one thing. In Matthew Chapter 7, when Jesus summarized all the Law and all the Prophets, do you know what he said?"

I looked at the ladies. I waited in case someone knew the Bible verse. They leaned in. You could have heard a pin drop. I told them, "Jesus said, 'Treat others the way you want to be treated.'[1] That's really what we're doing here. We're learning how to treat our kids the way we want to be treated."

One of the moms called me later and said, "I want to paint that phrase all over my house! My family needs to learn to treat each other the way we want to be treated."

"Yes," I said.

If I don't clean the toilets, I don't want my phone taken away from me. If I lie to my husband, I don't want to be slapped across the face. If the dishes need doing, I don't want to be yelled at—ever.

It's sad that many of us were raised in houses where we weren't treated with kindness. As kids we felt unsafe and unloved a lot of the time. But we're changing that for ourselves and for our kids, and we're changing it for our grandkids and great-grandkids, too.

Bad things happen, like kids being treated poorly. We don't know why bad things happen (theologians have been wrestling with the question for ages), but it seems to me that bad things happen when we forget that God, that love, is at the center of life. When God isn't at the center of life, life gets out of whack. When God's placed back at the center, values like self-control, kindness, and joy appear.[2]

I've seen hundreds of people make this transformation as they realign with their values. There's a tipping point where they don't feel annoyed as often. They have more positive thoughts than negative ones. They become clear on their boundaries and hurting people isn't okay anymore. Love comes into focus, and loving people is easier. Loving themselves is easier too. The loving focus helps them understand their values and prioritize their time. Not only that, but their eyes open to others who have that loving focus. When that happens, people who have known me send me links to books, articles, and other people they bump into who are like me. They meet new friends who also treat their children with kindness.

It's like that lyric from *Amazing Grace*, "I once was lost but now am found, was blind but now I see." I once was lost about how to treat myself and my children with dignity and respect. I once was blind to all the people who have already learned how to do it too.

Remember when I talked about the two big bubbles, one where people yell at their kids and the one where people don't? This is what breaking out of the yelling bubble looks like. At the beginning of the book, I said that I didn't know why I woke up one day and decided to do something about the yelling. But when I think about God, it's like God knew and whispered in my ear, "It's time to heal."

Healing for me meant learning to treat others the way I want to be treated. When I imagine God dreaming, I believe that's what God dreams for us all. He sees each of us at our brightest—our best self.

I want you to experience little pieces of your best self. That's why I have you celebrating, dancing in your kitchen, and giving yourself hugs. You know what it feels like to be the loving mom you want to be; you've done it many times when you've held your kids close, sung them a song, or put a Band-Aid on their booboo. This book is about expanding those best parts of you so you can experience feeling good more often, and walk through that door you're knocking on (and that door is closer than you think).

When Jesus started his ministry, he said, "The kingdom of God is at hand."[3] God's right here. Right here with you. God's breathing like a big mama lion waiting patiently for you, her sweet daughter, to breathe, too. When you yell, God's holding you like a mother holds her upset child. God's praying, wishing, and waiting patiently for you to heal.

Everything you need to heal is available. All you need to do is knock—to ask—and receive.

I earned a Masters in Divinity from the Episcopal Seminary of the Southwest in Austin. Sometimes people ask me about how God and religion fit into this work, helping families who want to stop the yelling. So now you know. This is my ministry.

Did you know "Mister Rogers," Fred, was a Lutheran pastor? I'm like a Mister Rogers for moms. Mister Rogers taught kids how to feel feelings in healthy ways. That's what I do for adults, but I take it one step further to use feelings to identify values and live by them. When I see a family break free of the yelling habit and live closer to the values of love and kindness, I see them as living closer to God's dream for their lives.

Chapter 31

Is It Strict?

A mom called me a "pansy" one day. She had the assumption my gentle parenting meant I wasn't strict or that the kids weren't respectful to me. She said, "I have a strict household where I expect my teenagers to treat everyone with respect and kindness, even strangers. All I have to do to get my kids to obey me is threaten to take their cell phones away, and they do whatever I ask them to do."

I could analyze her story for you, but I simply suggest you read the quote again and think about what she said and analyze her story for yourself. (My heart goes out to her— remember I believe everyone's doing the best they can.)

I want to be clear: I am strict and firm. My house is very strict but not in the traditional sense. Not in the sense that I threaten the kids, and they immediately hop up and obey me. My children do what I ask them to do, not out of fear, but because they feel safe, loved, and connected to me. They do it just because I ask them to, just as I will often happily do what they ask me to do, too.

At our house, there are firm boundaries. We are strictly kind and respectful. If a neighbor kid comes over and tries to get someone else in trouble, I talk with them about how in our house, no one gets in trouble. We talk about our feelings, we apologize if we've been hurtful, and we talk about how to do it better next time.

In our house, I'm strict. Even in my own actions, I require myself to be kind. When I'm unkind, I've crossed the line, and it's time for me to step back and apologize.

I am firm in the belief that what's important is treating others the way we want to be treated. So my kids contribute to the household. They help out around the house—not out of fear, but because we are a family that values each other. We treat each other the way we want to be treated. So we're happy to work together (most of the time).

Our family values are strict. We respect our bodies, hearts, and minds. We respect our home and the things in it. We respect our school and our neighborhood. We respect our neighbors, teachers, and friends. We respect the food we eat and the earth we live on.

In the old kind of strictness, there was a lot of stress. In this kind of strictness, there is breathing and grace—a lot of grace. In the old kind of strictness, it was the surface-level happiness of the parents that mattered most. In this kind of strictness, it's building loving relationships within the whole family that matter most.

Chapter 32

The Stages of Getting Help

I grew up in a family where you didn't ask for help. You didn't admit you needed help. Our family needed to look perfect, so getting help from someone outside the family was unacceptable because we needed to maintain the appearance of perfection.

I became an adult who didn't know I needed help. I was yelling at my kids without realizing there was a different way to do things, without understanding I needed help. Then, I threw the banana bread at Dad.

Getting help ended up being a challenge. Given how I was raised—to pull myself up by my own bootstraps and maintain the appearance of perfection—I was embarrassed to get help. The thought of getting help terrified me. I was afraid of getting in trouble and admitting all my messy mistakes. Getting help was also challenging because the people in my life weren't used to me asking for help.

Initially, I asked for help and no one heard me. My family was used to asking me for help, not the other way around. I had to dig my heels in and say, "No, I'm the one who needs help this time." To get all the help I needed, I had to look outside my family and friends.

At the end of this book, I'm going to teach you the stages of getting help.

1. Recognize you need help. This is big.
2. Ask for help. This is also big.
3. Get the help you need. It might be hard to find at first. Keep going. Find good helpers.
4. Receive the help you asked for, meaning do what the helpers tell you to do. This takes practice, and humility.

In an emotionally intelligent house, people ask for and get help. If you're a yeller and you want to stop yelling at your kids, you need help. This isn't something you can do alone. At the very least, you'll need the help of your husband and your kids. They can tell you when you need to take a break and breathe, if you're willing to listen.

By the way, you're more likely to succeed if you get more help. You may need a whole team of support.

First, I suggest finding a friend who yells at their kids and also wants to stop. Study this book together. Be each other's accountability partners. You're much more likely to succeed with an accountability partner. Statistically, "People are sixty-five percent likely to meet a goal after committing to another person. Their changes or success increase to ninety-five percent when they build in ongoing meetings with their partners to check in on their progress."[1]

In this quote, they're talking about entrepreneurs, but this is true for moms who want to stop yelling and have emotionally intelligent households. Share stories. Be sad together when you slip up and yell again. Celebrate together when you have success. Laugh through the whole messy process.

Second, you and your friend can find professional support—a coach or a counselor who will work on this issue with each of you individually. Find someone who has overcome this issue in his or her family or who was raised in an emotionally intelligent home. You'll learn so much from someone who has an outside perspective, someone who doesn't live in a family that yells at or threatens each other.

I knew a mom who went to see a counselor and said, "I want to stop yelling at my kids."

The counselor replied, "Everyone yells at their kids."

This isn't true. Remember the two bubbles, one where people yell and the one where they don't. You want a counselor who fits in the bubble of people who don't yell. This counselor didn't yet know about that bubble and wouldn't be a good mentor for a mom who wants to stop the yelling.

My biggest accountability partner has been my sister. We both started getting professional help around the same time. We've talked throughout the entire journey—crying over our hardships and celebrating our wins. We follow healthy parenting people on Instagram and tag each other in posts we like.

Third, remember that yelling is a habit, like smoking. It's a habit of the mind and body. A coach or counselor will help you work on the mind, but you'll want someone who can help you relieve stress in your body, too. Examples include massage therapists, physical therapists, and perhaps nutritionists. Work with people who can help relieve the stress in your body.

Over the years, I've gone through phases with different helpers. At first, I asked for help with my daughter's tantrums. We saw a counselor, a physical therapist, a doctor, and eventually settled on a massage therapist that specializes in releasing stress in the nervous system.

For myself, I've had help from teachers, coaches, counselors, doctors, massage therapists, and a nutritionist. I continue to see a counselor every week. I also eat healthy and exercise. I guard my sleep. I get massages when I'm feeling a lot of stress. I also have other mentors, people I can learn from who have what I want. I've had several mentors help me build my business.

So first, recognize your need for help. Second, ask for help. Third, find good partners, helpers, and mentors.

Having mentors is the best way to learn. To learn from a mentor, read their words, listen to them talk, watch their videos, and finally, spend time with them if you can. You learn more from talking with them on the phone, seeing them in person, or watching a video because not only do you read their words, you hear the way they speak and see their body language. At best, you can also experience the way they treat you. You learn volumes more these other ways rather than just reading. For example, when I buy non-fiction audio books, I try to buy ones that are read by the author, so I can be one step closer to them and absorb more of what they have to offer as a teacher, by listening to their voice.

If this book speaks to you, I'm probably a good mentor for you. To follow me as an author and receive invites to online classes, phone calls, and live events, subscribe on my website:

jeanettehargreaves.com

You'll have opportunities to meet other parents that are part of this parenting movement too—parents who are saying goodbye to yelling. They're done threatening kids with if/then statements, "If you do this, then you'll get punished," or "If you do this, then you'll get a reward." These parents are working on raising respectful kids who obey not out of fear, but because they feel safe and loved, and they feel a part of the family. We're realigning with our family values, not only for the good of our own children, but also for our children's children, to benefit generations.

Chapter 33

At the End of this Book

Read this book again. Get out your highlighter and highlight parts that stand out to you. Circle things. Host a book club and read it with a group. Invite me to join the book club one time; I can do it on speakerphone.

Write the sticky notes and put them around the house. Print the PDFs and read them together with your family. Follow the steps.

These techniques work.

The other day I realized that I hadn't yelled and lost control with the kids in over a year. It's not in my mama tool belt anymore. And I thought to myself, "It would be cool to get a one-year celebration certificate or some kind of token to commemorate 'No More Yelling.'" I know how difficult this journey can be, so let's celebrate. When you get to the point when you haven't yelled in over a month, email me and let me know. I'll send you a certificate, just for fun:

jeanette@tempercoaching.com

BONUS

When Mama Yells

A poem to read to your kids after you yell

When mama yells, she's feeling sad. Or stressed. Or angry.

Or maybe she's feeling helpless and scared.

There's a lot of big feelings inside your mama,

And she hasn't yet learned how to feel them.

She hasn't learned how to say, "Hey, that hurt my feelings
And I feel sad."

Or, "Hey, mama's tired right now and needs to take a Break."

I'm sorry baby. I love you.

I learned how to yell from my mom or dad.

But I'm getting help.

And I'm working on getting better.

I'm learning how to feel my feelings in healthy ways.

I'm learning how to be helpful and happy.

I'm learning how to have a safe and loving home.

For you, for Daddy, and for me, too.

I love you baby.

I'm working on it.

It's not your fault.

And it's not your job to fix me.

Other grown-ups are helping me,

And it's going to be all right.

We've got it under control.

The grown-ups are doing their jobs.

And your job is to be a kid.

To have fun.

And together we're going to learn how to feel all our Feelings.

The sad ones, the happy ones, the scared ones, and the angry

Ones, too.

And we're going to feel our feelings in healthy ways.

We're learning how to be helpful,

How to be healthy,

How to be happy.

I'm sorry, baby.

I love you.

Now go on your happy way.

The Sticky Notes

If you wrote out all the sticky notes, there are twenty of them. I didn't write a sticky note for Chapter 13 titled, "The Husband." You get to decide for yourself if you married a good man. If you did, you might make yourself a "Daddy do" sticky note, and let daddy do what he does.

1. Anger is powerful. I can be helpful or hurtful with it.
2. Yelling is a habit you can break.
3. Who will I tell? I'm a yeller and I want to stop yelling.
4. I'm in the second stage of learning. It's painful not knowing, but I will learn.
5. Where do I feel anger in my body? What does it feel like?
6. Mama lions YAWN.
7. I'm feeling . . . (This is a list of feeling words or you can use the Feelings for the Fridge PDF).
8. I'm safe and I can handle this feeling.
9. What is the good news in my life?
10. What roles do I play in my family? Do I have to play those roles? If not, can I cut myself free?
11. I'm feeling stressed. I'm safe. I'm loved. And I can handle it. (Yawn.)
12. They did the best they could. I did the best I could. And now, I'll do better.

13. Who do I "should?"

14. What are they telling me? What am I telling them with my behavior?

15. I'm sorry. I care about you. I'll try not to do it again. / Thank you. I care about you too.

16. Think about the Redo

17. Celebrate the pushback.

18. Hold on! You can do it! No new projects.

19. What can I do to feel good today and better tomorrow?

20. What's the surface issue? What's the feeling underneath?

The PDF Links

Here are the hidden pages on my website so you can print the PDFs for use at home.

jeanettehargreaves.com/feelings

jeanettehargreaves.com/values

jeanettehargreaves.com/connect

Acknowledgments

Thank you to all the people, known and unknown, who have been waiting and praying, rooting me on as I finish this book. It's been a journey.

Thank you to the woman from Adult Protective Services who came out to interview me about throwing the banana bread; you were gentle and kind.

A special thanks to my mentors and the folks who took a chance on me. The Very Rev. Cynthia Briggs Kittredge, Rev. Kathleen Russell, Dr. Claire Colombo, Rev. Mary Wilson, Kathleen Clawson, Chris Jackson, Rebecca Hall, Laine Young, Allison Roper, David Cantu, Bridget Brandt, and Jenny Shih.

Thank you to my own personal therapists. Also, thank you to the therapists in the referral network for my program.

I'm thankful for all the people I've talked with about my coaching, people who have interviewed me about my work, and people who have hired me for coaching and come to my events. I've learned so much from you. Thank you. You all have made me a better coach.

The inspiration for my ideas came from many sources, as Ecclesiastes 1:9 says, "There is nothing new under the sun." This is simply my version of things that have been taught by many teachers over the generations. I will try to give credit to the sources I recognize, but I won't remember them all. There may be words and phrases you've heard elsewhere, or if you're a friend of mine, there's a chance one of your own ideas stuck in the back of my brain until it came up again, and because I adopted it as one of my own—thank you and apologies for the lack of credit due.

I've also noticed my own ideas reflected back to me from other places, many of us with similar backgrounds have similar experiences and congruent ideas arise. For example, I came up with the idea for the "Redo," and then I learned about Dr. Becky Bailey's technique in *Conscious Discipline* called "Take Two." It's the same idea, just different words. I recently discovered *Conscious Discipline*, and it's one source of inspiration for me. While I've never been trained in "Conscious Discipline," I follow the organization on Instagram, and sometimes, I listen to their podcasts. Their teachings are some of the most elevated I've run across, especially when it comes to discipline in the classroom and ideas for school administration. I'm also inspired by Big Life Journal, a growth mindset group for parents who received their foundational ideas from the work of Carol Dweck, PhD. My training in seminary by Dr. David Jones in family emotional systems also had an impact. He is the professor who told me the story about his kids and the ice cream. I continued to learn and read about family systems long after I received my degree because knowing about systems helps you break habits. I also enjoy following the work of the Emotional Intelligence Network Six Seconds.

As a former news producer, I'm inspired by the teachings at the Solutions Journalism Network. The research by Timothy D. Wilson and James W. Pennebaker, Ph.D. around transformational storytelling has also been inspirational. It's unclear who originated the "Four Stages of Learning," but Noel Burch, as an employee of Gordon Training International, created the Conscious Competence Ladder in 1970 that represents the stages I talk about. The little book called *Recovery: A Guide for Adult Children of Alcoholics* by Herbert L. Gravitz and Julie D. Bowden is another one of my sources for inspiration.

Austin Montessori School, where my kids attended preschool, taught me quite a few things, such as the cycle of activity, how to limit screen time for the benefit of the family, how to select quality literature for my children's library, and that it was okay to have toys without batteries in them. They also taught me how to have compassion for children—to teach them instead of punish.

I learned a lot during my training to become a public school teacher at the Region XIII Education Service Center in

Texas. That's where I first learned to focus on what you want instead of what you don't want. That was life changing for me.

I also learned a lot while working for St. Richard's Episcopal Church. I grew as the families and teens I worked with grew. I'm thankful for the training I received from the Diocese of Texas during that time and the support of Ewart Jones, Jr. That community supported my first program, "Integrity Online: Safety's Not Enough."

Thank you to the people who are out there doing this work alongside me, helping many parents become better parents. Thank you also to the many parents who did this work before me, who paved the way for people like myself.

Thanks to vocem, LLC and my patient editor, Cortney Donelson. Thanks also to photographer Will Gallagher of Gallagher Studios who took pictures for the cover.

Thank you to my friends for inspiring me and believing in me. I love you dearly (you know who you are). Love and thanks to my sister, Catherine. I love you to the moon. Thanks to my kids—my sweethearts. And special thanks to my husband, Geoff. Love you, honey.

Notes

Chapter 4

1. Stanford Alumni, "Developing a Growth Mindset with Carol Dweck," YouTube, https://www.youtube.com/watch?v=hiiEeMN7vbQ.

Chapter 5

1. Lauri Nummenmaa, Enrico Glerean, Riitta Hari, and Jari K. Hietanen, "Bodily Maps of Emotions," Proceedings of the National Academy of Sciences of the United States of America 111 (January 2014) https://www.pnas.org/content/111/2/646.

Chapter 6

1. The Emotional Intelligence Network Six Seconds, "Why 'Six Seconds'? The Inside Story & Neuroscience Behind Our Intriguing Name," https://www.6seconds.org/2019/06/19/why-six-seconds-about-our-intriguing-name/.

Chapter 8

1. Hans Rosling, Factfulness: *Ten Reasons We're Wrong About the World and Why Things Are Better Than You Think*, Flatiron Books New York, 2018, chapter 8.

2. Matthew 7:7, NIV.

Chapter 9

1. Edwin H. Friedman, *Friedman's Fables*, The Guilford Press New York, 2014, "The Bridge."

Chapter 11

1. Conscious Discipline, "365 Days of Conscious Discipline (Perpetual Flip Calendar)," February 21.

Chapter 21

1. Dr. Becky Bailey, *Conscious Discipline: Building Resilient Classrooms Expanded and Updated Edition*, Loving Guidance, Inc. Florida, 2015, "Chapter 2: Brain State Model."

Chapter 30

1. Matthew 7:12, my own translation.

2. Self-control, kindness and joy are listed as some of the fruits of the Spirit in Galatians 5:22-23.

3. Mark 1:15, NKJV.

Chapter 32

1. Barret Wissman, "An Accountability Partner Makes You Vastly More Likely to Succeed," Entrepreneur (March 20, 2018) https://www.entrepreneur.com/article/310062.